The Female Paradigm

The Female Paradigm

An Idea Whose Time Has Come

Ignacio Iriarte
and
Alexander Iriarte

Copyright © 2011 by Ignacio Iriarte and Alexander Iriarte.

ISBN: Softcover   978-1-4568-8174-0
           Ebook   978-1-4568-8175-7

All rights reserved. No part of this book may be reproduced or transmitted in any form or by any means, electronic or mechanical, including photocopying, recording, or by any information storage and retrieval system, without permission in writing from the copyright owner.

This book was printed in the United States of America.

To order additional copies of this book, contact:
Xlibris Corporation
1-888-795-4274
www.Xlibris.com
Orders@Xlibris.com

Contents

Acknowledgments 7

Connections—An Overview of the Book 9

Introduction 13

Preface 19

Chapter 1—Sexism: The Curse of Humanity
                (An Historical Perspective) 27

Chapter 2—Education Versus The "Idiot" Factory 72

Chapter 3—Health Care and Overpopulation:
                How Much Does a Life Cost? 89

Chapter 4—Energy: The Ecological Imperative 99

Chapter 5—Prejudice: The Price of Ignorance
                (Racism and Ethnocentrism) 104

Chapter 6—International Relations: The Beautiful American 117

Chapter 7—Values, Religion, and Culture 134

Chapter 8—Globalization and Nationalism 142

Chapter 9—Social Evolution 164

Conclusion 169

Acknowledgments

To all the women throughout history whom have contributed to bring compassion, love, and peace to humanity.

We would like to thank the architect and economist Doroteo A. Rodriguez who offered his knowledge, expertise and critical evaluation in different areas of this book. Our gratitude also goes to Sally Marsh Kilic for her important role editing The Female Paradigm.

Connections

An Overview of the Book

This book postulates that:

By replacing our planet's aggressive, male-dominated paradigm with a nurturing, female - dominated one, the resources that we now expend on our global military could, instead, be used for tangible social and economic progress.

By using our limited funds (that are presently dedicated to military budgets) for education in conjunction with the help of technology, the following solutions could be implemented:

1. Provide reliable and accessible birth control to the global community in order to reduce population growth, which will have the concomitant effect of diminishing:

   Poverty
   Disease
   Unemployment
   Hunger
   Crime
   Pollution
   Uncontrollable and conflictive migration

2. Provide education and programs for citizens so that they can participate, learn, and practice the fundamental principles of democracy and community service.
3. Teach and practice tolerance and respect in order to understand the roots, problems, and negative consequences of racism, sexism, ethnocentrism, and religious intolerance.
4. Understand our energy and ecological crisis and actively work on solutions.
5. Understand globalization and the positive and negative consequences of it, not only for ourselves, but also for the rest of the world, in order to develop a win/win formula.
6. Improve international relations based upon cooperation rather than unfair Darwinian competition.
7. Prioritize our values and move away from extreme materialism and superficial relationships.
8. Understand and respect others' religions, which will promote peace.
9. Practice nationalism by elevating our moral virtues without denegrating other nations; then lead by example.
10. Offer universal and affordable health care to all citizens of the world.

To summarize the connection or chain reaction that would occur, given this set of circumstances, we could argue that:

1. By replacing most of the male (aggressive) world leaders with female (nurturing) leaders the following positive changes could occur:

    a. Most females would reduce or exchange military budgets for social programs budgets.
    b. The implementation of beneficial educational, nutritional, and health care programs, could help to reduce the extent of the global problems of overpopulation, pollution, poverty, and unemployment.

    c. Fewer people on the planet would result in less pollution, poverty, and national and international conflicts, and more jobs would be available.

2. Educating the disenfranchised people of the world would allow them to participate in the economic and political decisions that affect them and their future generations.

Introduction

From an historical perspective, we argue that since the beginning of time, males have done a very poor job as leaders of societies. Since recorded history, more than fourteen thousand wars have been fought on this planet, and the level of destruction, waste, and human suffering is incalculable. We believe that by replacing most of the male world leaders with female leaders, we could solve or drastically reduce many of the problems afflicting humanity. We propose that females (with their less aggressive nature) could manage to replace the obscene amount of energy and resources used for weapons and military purposes in exchange for social and educational programs that would solve world problems, such as poverty and famine, and promote peace.

In Chapter 1 Sexism

We present an historical review of the literature about the different degrees of sexism and its relationship to technological and scientific development. We explain that the physical or biological differences between males and females (even though they played an important role in history) are no longer relevant in our modern, technological world. By using cross-cultural analysis, we show that within the spectrum of human cultures, the practice of sexism is one of the most controversial and conflictive ones. The gap between the Scandinavian (modern and liberated) roles for women versus some of the Middle Eastern (ancient and oppressive) roles for women is one of the fundamental elements for the clash of civilizations of our present times. We also suggest that, to different degrees, males all over the world are fighting to preserve the power that traditionally, by force, they have enjoyed throughout history.

In Chapter 2 Education and Leadership

If the financial resources expended on military budgets could be appropriated for education and social programs, tremendous positive changes would be possible. We explain and emphasize the importance of education in order to achieve real, tangible changes at both national and international levels. We believe that ignorance and misinformation are the roots of many social evils, such as racism, sexism, and ethnocentrism. The solution to a majority of the world's problems is education at all levels, from the President of the United States to the illiterate of third world countries. A multicultural, pragmatic education in which critical thinking skills are used to understand and solve our local, national, and international problems (without using our ethnocentric filters and obstacles) is imperative. We also suggest that an important part of our education systems be focused on citizen participation so that from a very early age, individuals learn how to be active members of their societies and to practice democratic principles.

In Chapter 3 Health Care and Overpopulation

We make the connection between the uses of funds (that would ordinarily have been spent on the military and are now spent on education and social programs) and the solutions to the problems of overpopulation and lack of health care for many regions of the world. By seriously dealing with overpopulation through sex education and global health care, we will reduce or alleviate many other problems, such as malnutrition, poverty, and pollution.

We also suggest that if there is one thing that should not be commercialized, it should be health care. It is immoral (and should be illegal) for health care facilities, pharmaceutical companies, and insurance companies to take advantage of people's infirmities and suffering to make obscene profits. We believe that the money that could be saved by eliminating the business aspect of health care could not only drastically reduce the national debt in the U.S. and many other nations, but it could also help families and individuals reduce their financial burdens and psychological stresses.

In Chapter 4 Energy and Ecology

We believe that the entropic nature of the military/industrial complex is responsible for part of the energy and ecological problems that we confront in our times. Implementation of the female paradigm may allow for serious international disarmament. The waste of resources used and needed to build and operate the global military sector is one of the reasons why many nations do not have enough money to take care of their people's basic needs, such as food, education, and health care. The strategic, geo-political justification for international competition and intervention could be eliminated by using the wasteful military resources in the development and implementation of alternative sources of energy, such as solar, wind, bio-mass, and many other sources of energy less contaminating and more accessible to most countries of the world.

In Chapter 5 Prejudice, Racism, and Ethnocentrism

The roots of most forms of prejudices, such as racism, are ignorance and false stereotypes that still exist in most societies. The solution to most of these problems in our societies is education. By teaching people that the differences between humans are so insignificant that it is irrational to continue to divide people based upon a few superficial physical differences, we could eliminate racism from the planet.

In Chapter 6 International Relations

We explain that the traditional, conflictive, male paradigm, with its eternal power struggle between nations or regions, could be replaced by a cooperative, female paradigm which would drastically reduce the need for absurd military budgets. We suggest that the U.S. could not only be the economic leader of the world but also the moral one by practicing freedom and democracy both at home and overseas. By showing the beauty of the American people, instead of the ugliness of some of the political leaders who have misrepresented the great United States of America, positive change will follow. By having an international judicial system in which everyone (including political leaders) will be accountable for their crimes without the protection of presidential pardons or national sovereignty, we will create a valid and reliable system for other countries to emulate.

In Chapter 7 Values, Culture, and Religion

Most religions preach the same fundamental principles of love, peace, and compassion. The problem is that the gap between preaching and practicing is too great to seriously achieve the espoused goals of these great religions. Comparative religious studies that concentrate on the positive similarities among the world's major religions are one way that we humans can advance in our social and moral quest. Our modern, egocentric, materialistic culture is creating conflicts and divisions between different societies when we should be striving to develop connections which decrease tensions.

In Chapter 8 Globalization and Nationalism

In our ever-changing, modern, technological world, the international dependency and inter-dependency between countries should be designed to create a win-win formula in which the less developed countries have a chance to compete and prosper, instead of falling further and further behind, economically and socially. With the protection of the traditional concept of Intellectual Property Rights, the developed nations are practicing a "Darwinian Globalization," which will only widen the gap between first and third world countries. We believe that if American female leaders practice and implement democratic and fair principles, that globalization can be based upon cooperation and welfare for all, instead of competition and subjugation (the products of man-made, international relations and economic institutions). If the U.S. takes the leadership role and promotes fair interactions, then most of the nations of the world will prefer to deal with this beautiful side of America.

In Chapter 9 Social Evolution

Most people would probably agree that education is the most effective and useful tool to advance social, economic, and human development. In this book, we have attempted to explain how, through education, we could solve some of the major problems afflicting humanity, such as overpopulation, poverty, sexism, racism, and many other problems which have their roots in ignorance. In this chapter, we go beyond solving those problems and express the belief that all of humanity could learn to be more "civilized" or more peaceful and tolerant of individual's differences. We could evolve as humans by teaching the importance of genuine spiritual values versus the emptiness of the materialistic culture, and the value of time for human relations versus time spent at work in order to buy more material things. We could even teach new concepts, ideas, or words that would make it the norm to be more nurturing and tolerant, and less egocentric and envious—in other words, to be better humans.

Preface

"All the forces in the world are not so powerful as an idea whose time has come." Victor Hugo

In the 21st century, an idea's time has, indeed, come—the idea that our world may be greatly improved if we place women in positions of leadership so that they may use the female personality traits of compassion, nurturing, cooperation, empathy, and other humanistic characteristics to create a better world. Until this point in human history, men have ruled the world and imposed destructive forces to do so. It is time for men to step aside so that women can lay their gentle hands upon the earth.

The two main components of this book include:

1. The roles that females should play in positions of political/economic/social leadership in order to achieve a more humanitarian and peaceful world
2. The importance of education to realistically implement the necessary changes to achieve the first goal

It would be difficult to understand the logic behind the potential for change and progress without presenting an historical perspective of the role that males and females have played throughout the centuries. For millennia, male dominance over females has limited the human potential to achieve a higher level of social engineering that could drastically reduce the amount of violence, wars, and destruction on our planet.

Based on the premise that males are more violent and aggressive than females, we could argue that if we humans want a more peaceful and better world, we should establish democratic systems in as many countries as possible. Then we must educate the populace about the necessity of electing as many females as possible to act as political leaders who will work for a peaceful and prosperous world for the majority of people in our future generations.

The idea of a utopian world may be unrealistic, but the realistic possibility to make drastic changes for a more ideal world is within our power. Males have had a long tenure as the world's power brokers and have had ample opportunity to create a better world. However, all one need do is look at the hopeless plight of billions of people on this planet to realize that males have created more problems than they have offered solutions to address human misery. The number one, and most negative, legacy of man is the manifestation of thousands of wars that have been perpetrated by men throughout human history.

If we take as the definition of intelligence "the ability to make connections in order to solve problems or questions," we could argue that some of the most serious problems confronting humanity, such as violence, hunger, poverty, and global warming, among others, could be solved by intelligent and moral actions. Males have misused the world's natural, financial, and human resources throughout history in their quest for power and money. These same resources would most likely have been used in more intelligent and humanitarian ways by females toward solving problems (instead of creating them) for our already fragile global community, because females seem to have a proclivity to create and nurture life, rather than to exploit and destroy it.

Collectively, entire nations, behave abysmally when it comes to human relations; our nations' leaders have convinced their peoples that our main priority for our capital resources should be appropriations for weapons systems which will allow us to conquer and exploit the world's limited resources so that we can continually improve our materialistic standard of living, instead of expending those resources on providing for basic human needs. As a result, much of the world's population lives in abject poverty with substandard living conditions, while those who have excelled in weapons technology have excessive material wealth and seemingly no conscious about what they have done to humanity to maintain their standard of living.

With the billions of dollars that nations spend on their military capabilities, many of the world's problems could be solved by using those same resources in intelligent, humanitarian ways. For example, with the money that it costs to buy a tank (which could only be used for two things: to destroy and kill, or to be stored until it becomes obsolete), we could build many schools which would benefit millions of children. Those children could, in turn, improve living conditions for future generations in their countries, resulting in exponentially beneficial effects on humanity.

The main idea of this book is to encourage all who read it to replace historically, male-created military budgets with new, female-created humanitarian budgets devoted to educational and social programs that promote peace and understanding among the citizens of the world. If we implement budgets devoted to improving the human condition, rather than to exploiting and destroying people, we can potentially move toward a more peaceful and just world. If one accepts the premise that females are more devoted to nurturing and improving life, then it follows that placing females into positions of political/economic/social power will result in the expenditure of resources to achieve a higher level of civilization.

By making the connection between the different aspects and problems confronting our modern and complex world, we will explain how exchanging the traditional, male-dominated, aggressive paradigm with a female-dominated, nurturing paradigm, will be a great leap forward in achieving social and spiritual evolution on our delicate planet. Starting with the premise that females would be more willing to solve conflicts without violence, it stands to reason that they would, therefore, drastically reduce military budgets and then devote financial resources toward the goal of achieving international cooperation necessary to deal with the main problems afflicting humanity. These dozen problems include:

1. Mal-distribution of food resources
2. Inadequate health care and education
3. Overpopulation
4. Depletion of energy sources
5. Contamination of our environment
6. Racism, sexism, and ethnocentrism
7. Migration restrictions
8. Conflictive and destructive international relations
9. Unfair and inefficient criminal justice systems
10 Hypocritical and selfish moral values
11. A Darwinian approach to globalization
12. A pervasive culture of materialism and envy

After an historical perspective and review of the literature, we will explore each one of these problems with the intention of presenting viable solutions that realistically could be implemented by utilizing our educational institutions, the latest technology, and (most importantly) moral leaders.

The possible solutions or arguments presented in this book initially may seem unrealistic or impossible to achieve. However, if one reads with an open mind and a positive outlook, the solutions may seem more plausible than they were at first consideration. If one carefully observes the precepts of the world's major religions, including Christianity, Judaism, Islam, Buddhism, and Hinduism, one realizes that the concepts of love, peace, compassion, and brother/sisterhood (the main goals of these religions) are naturally the goals for which any honest, moral, decent individual should strive. Unfortunately, organized religious institutions frequently hinder many people's efforts to achieve these desired virtues. There have been some instances in history when adherents of these major religions have been able to live or co-exist in harmony and peace. An excellent example is found in the city of Toledo, Spain, where, for hundreds of years, followers of Islam, Christianity, and Judaism tolerated, coexisted, and respected each other. The basic formula for their success was practicing The Golden Rule: "Do unto others as you would have others do unto you."

In this book, we are presenting a number of steps that are interrelated and can lead to a more just and harmonious world. With more action and fewer words, it should be possible to solve most of the major problems that are affecting the people of the world today. It is difficult, but not impossible, to change the status quo. The argument that many people have—that it is too idealistic or impossible to create a utopian society—is either an excuse manufactured by the people in power who are against change, or the result of a lack of honest, moral, and pragmatic political and religious leaders. As stated before, males have had millennia to make positive changes and to practice their expressed beliefs, yet after thousands of wars and unquantifiable human suffering, mankind is no better off than before. If the people of the world are serious about real social and political change, then it is time for females (with their nurturing instinct) to take the helm of political leadership and to navigate us to, perhaps not a utopian society, but at least to a first-rate society in which each individual has the opportunity to fully develop his or her human potential.

It is difficult to fight against tradition and the economic interests that benefit the people who are already in power. It is also difficult to challenge the weapons industries' financial and political strength or the major pharmaceutical and insurance companies' inordinate political influence purchased by their obscenely lucrative profits. However, it is possible, using the tools of education, democracy, and technology, to elect courageous and moral leaders who would be willing to work for change. Instead of having chauvinistic, power-hungry, male leaders deciding and controlling the future of nations and the global community, the people of the world need to unite in their efforts to place into power female leaders with universal, beneficial views about how to solve the world's problems. Popular examples of women who work to improve the world (though not elected, political leaders), and whom many consider good role models, include, Mother Theresa, Oprah Winfrey, Salma Hayek, Queen Noor, and Angelina Jolie. All of these women have engaged in humanitarian efforts to make life better for many people on this planet. What if the world was lead by women like these and other females who understand the priority of serving the needs of human beings versus the blind concept of the Darwinian "survival of the fittest" model? As Mother Theresa once said, "If we have no peace, it is because we have forgotten that we belong to each other." Think of the potential for positive change in our world if we had in power someone like Eleanor Roosevelt who changed the role of the First Lady of the United States forever.

> "She held press conferences, wrote a newspaper column every day, and had a radio show in which she expressed opinions on social problems and causes, such as racism, bigotry, child labor, and world peace. She traveled the globe, raising money for UNICEF on behalf of children in need, and became a delegate three times and chair to the United Nations Commission on Human Rights. Mrs. Roosevelt was first lady of the World."[1]

The following diagrams present a logical and simple explanation of the relationship between the historically, male-dominated world and its problems, and the potentially female-governed world with its solutions:

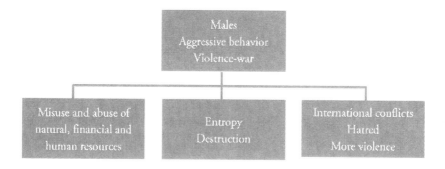

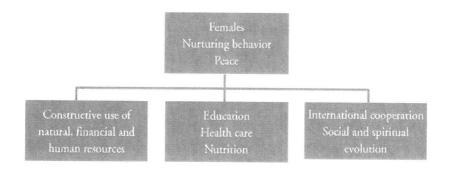

Chapter 1

Sexism

Throughout history, the concept of sexism and sexual stereotyping has more or less prevailed among human cultures. Today in the 21st century, some societies, such as the Scandinavians, have achieved a great level of change and progress toward the elimination of sexism. In the United States of America, some improvement has been made in the status of women, but there is still much to be done before we can claim that we have gender equality. On the other hand, in many countries of the world, sexism is as prevalent now as it was centuries ago.

In this chapter, we attempt to explain the level of sexism that best represents the majority of people in our multi-cultural world. In order to achieve this goal, we concentrate our explanations on research that was conducted in the 1960's and 1970's, since that is the time in human history that saw the most tangible change in sex roles. It is true that at the beginning of the 20th century, women gained the right to vote, and later on, women finally acquired reliable birth control methods with the invention of "the pill." However, in practice, it was not until the 1960's that women finally began to move forward toward achieving equal rights in the United States. Even today in the 21st century, we are exposed to the evils of sexism, as Bob Herbert described in the New York Times:

> "If there was ever a story that deserved more coverage by the news media, it's the dark persistence

of misogyny in America. Sexism, in its myriad destructive forms, permeates nearly every aspect of American life. For many men, it's the national pastime, much bigger than baseball or football."[2]

The fact that a great number of people live in very traditional and conservative societies deserves a psychological and sociological analysis of their background, as well as what their future holds as they are confronted with the knowledge and ideas of the modern, technological world. The fact that there are no longer excuses to rationalize the oppressive and unfair treatment of women is clearly explained by the 1960's and 1970's research. In a way, this research represents a landmark period of time which some societies (Scandinavians, for example) have surpassed and that many other societies (like some Middle Eastern nations) are nowhere near achieving. The extent of the progress that was made for gender equality in the United States and other developed countries in the 1960's can be drastically contrasted with the sad lack of progress for this change in most developing countries that, in many cases, are centuries behind in providing equality for the female sector of their societies.

Time line illustrating the progression from more to less sexism present in various societies:

Pre-history—Afghanistan (Middle East) / 1920's—Latin America/ 1960's—USA / 2010—Scandinavia.

(Historical Perspective)

In the spectrum of human history, no one single society or social behavior can be regarded as the ultimate representation of mankind. In each society, we assume and accept as 'masculine' and 'feminine' a series of fundamental concepts, which are basically defined by culture. Perhaps as Mead suggests, no form of social behavior is limited to a specific gender. All phenomena that occur in society are culturally defined.[3]

Progressively, during the last few decades, especially since the industrial revolution, a number of factors may have had transcendental effects on gender roles. Scientific developments, such as birth control, mechanization, mobility of society, mass education, and other technological elements may have produced significant change in our traditional views of gender roles and human sexuality [4]. Human behavior appears to be inextricably linked to biological make-up, as Burton points out:

> "The difficulty in analyzing man's behavior is that it is extremely complex and infinitely variable. He has broken away from biological necessity; he has his own patterns of behavior . . . however, our ancestors were still bound by biological laws and behavior in the way that was provided by natural selection as being in their best interest." [5]

The argument of biological determinism, which historically designated specific gender roles, is no longer logical or valid in our modern 21st century, where intellectual ability (and not biological differences) is the most important factor determining survival. According to the law of natural selection, humans, as any other species, have always had to adapt to new and different environments and circumstances in order to survive.[6] Men and women have created and changed a number of roles with specific purposes during specific periods of time. The role division of labor and activities has been decided by the individual's capabilities and the social structure which, up until this century, has had a direct relationship to the physiological constitution, or a person's physical strength.[7]

Due to the physiological differences between males and females, the traditional division of gender roles has been greatly determined by physical strength. Strength may be characterized by aggressiveness and power, which have been considered traditional male characteristics. Females, on the other hand, being the physically weaker gender, have had to take complimentary roles, adopting the characteristics of submissiveness. As Weiss suggested, since quality of performance depends greatly on the physical characteristics that relate to the amount of strength individuals have, women can be dealt with simply as "fractional men."[8] This archaic mentality was accepted by many (including many females) when physical strength made a difference in achieving certain goals more efficiently; however, in today's world, because of mechanical (technological) developments, male superior strength may no longer be a viable characteristic for determining the division of roles between males and females.

Not only is the degree of difference between the physical strength of males versus females difficult to measure, but it is even more difficult to know the real potential for most females' physical strength, since our cultural and esthetical values discourage the so-called "masculinization" of the female body. From Greek statues to modern fashion-model pictures, the ideal female body has been presented in a very limited and stereotypical way. In reality, females can perform any physical activity as well as males, if given the same opportunities, training, and (more importantly) motivation to do so. A good example of this artificial physiological gap between the genders is in the field of sports, where the differences in performance between males and females have become increasingly smaller with time.

Another very important element to be considered when studying the division of roles between the two sexes has been, and still is to some degree, the phenomenon of pregnancy, birth, and motherhood. A substantial amount of literature (Mead, D'Andeade, Frederickson) expresses what De Riencourt describes very clearly:

> "Hunting anthropoids had to provide for females and offspring in their new way of life. Menstruation, pregnancy, and the care of children were not compatible with the hunt, which thus became an exclusively male occupation, leaving females in charge of food gathering, whenever possible and convenient.[9]

The idea that females' reproductive roles are an impediment for participating in any or all activities of human endeavor belongs in the past. Since not every culture (for better or worse) has achieved the level of sophistication and technological development that the United States of America and other first world countries have, the traditional (primitive) view of female subordinated roles is still the norm in the majority of the global communities. The idea of equality among the genders is not only rejected in these cultures but is the source of conflicts between nations and cultures.

The changes produced by technological developments, particularly in the areas of biology and medicine, may have enabled us to control reproduction for the first time in human history. Developments, such as the birth-control pill and relatively safe abortion methods (although questionable), offer to our civilization the possibility of controlling population and the family dynamic. The most significant effect of "the pill" is that it has allowed humans a very acceptable and practical method of separating conception and reproduction from the act of sexual intercourse, and may, therefore, have a tremendous impact on our attitudes toward gender roles.

Our traditional views of sexual behavior may be challenged, as Jeanniere expressed it, "We have reached the stage where we need no longer leave births to the chance of amorous impulses . . . [in]semination can be selective."[10]

The number one reason for the cultural practice of sexism has, therefore, been potentially eliminated. By using education and reliable birth control, females now have greater choices and expanded roles in our societies. Hence, we can now move toward instituting fairer and more equalitarian practices in our societies. De Riencourt contends that the changes in attitudes towards sex roles is a consequence of technological developments, stating that

> "Urbanization, an inevitable consequence of the industrial revolution, was growing fast, along with an increasing division and specialization of labor, the invention of the typewriter, the rapid development of business offices, and the shift toward 'service'

> economies—all of which fostered in the early 1920's the 'emancipated' woman. The old patriarchal family disintegrated; 'extended' family ties loosened up with the increasing mobility of the population and the steady emigration out of rural areas and all of its built-in instability and rising divorce rate. Birth control became popular, releasing women's energies for other, still-undefined, purposes."[11]

What better purpose could there be for women than participating in the economic, social, and political arenas, in order to bring real changes into our chaotic and conflictive world?

The process of change to liberate females from oppressive (and often abusive) treatment by males has been long and slow, but now, with the help of education and technology, we can accelerate the real change that humanity has been waiting for—a change for justice and peace.

In the United States of America alone, with one of the most democratic governments in the world, it took more than a century from its creation for women to be granted the right to vote. With the birth of our nation in 1789, the voting right was strictly reserved for white, land-owning, educated, wealthy males. Later, this right was granted to all white males. After the Civil War ended in 1865, freed male slaves were granted this privilege. It was not until 1920 that women were included in the democratic process. Finally, an act of Congress in 1924 allowed Native Americans this cherished right. Realistically, only in the last few decades have females been getting involved and participating in the traditionally male-dominated world of politics. Since that is the case in the U.S., we can see how far behind are many other nations and regions of the world which are beginning to try to implement some type of democratic institutions. It is estimated that more than 85% of the political leaders worldwide are males, and for some nations, the obstacles for a woman to become a political leader are as big as they have always been.

The challenge for new generations is to break away from the subjugating concepts of the past and embrace the future with the power of knowledge. We must use education to understand and change the aggressive and violent behavior of the male-dominated paradigm and make it invalid. We must insist upon implementing more peaceful and productive ways to interact with each other.

A manifestation of this change can be exemplified by one of the new elements that is currently being dealt with in the realm of social psychology: the concept of "androgyny." As Singer described it, "Androgyny refers to a specific way of joining the "masculine" and "feminine" aspects of a single human being . . . we see much evidence of the trend toward androgyny in our Western world today in social customs, manners, and morals."[12]

According to Encarta Dictionary, and for the purpose of clarification, let's define the terms masculine, feminine, and androgyny:

Masculine (adjective)

1. of men and boys—relating or belonging to men and boys rather than women and girls
2. of traditional manly character—having traits or qualities traditionally associated with men or boys rather than women or girls

Feminine (adjective)

1. Conventionally associated with women—conventionally thought to be appropriate for a woman or girl
2. Attributed to women—considered to be characteristic of women

Androgynous (adjective)

Blending masculine and feminine qualities and characteristics

"Gender stereotypes," as defined by Myers, "are people's beliefs about how men and women behave. These stereotypes have been around for many years, and they continue to be strong in today's society. A major concern dealing with gender stereotypes are the effects they may have on leadership. Some research suggests that these stereotypes may present obstacles for women who wish to compete for leadership positions."[13]

Some studies describe fundamental differences between the genders as Hosoda and Stone found "78 overall attributes associated with males. Twelve of the 78 attributes were considered 'key' masculine attributes. These include: handsome, aggressive, tough, courageous, strong, forceful, arrogant, egotistical, boastful, hard-headed, masculine, and dominant. Sixty-two overall attributes were associated with females, and of these, nine were considered 'key' feminine attributes. These include: affectionate, sensitive, appreciative, sentimental, sympathetic, nagging, fussy, feminine, and emotional. This suggests that people believe that men and women generally behave differently from one another."[14]

Since some of the modern conflicts (especially in the Middle East) are based upon cultural and religious differences, it is important to understand, explore, and assess the relationship between societies with different levels of technological development and the gender roles of individuals living in those cultures. The concepts of masculinity and femininity have been part of the idiosyncrasy of all societies that we have known until now. As Mead explains, "In every known human society, everywhere in the world, the young male learns that when he grows up, one of the things which he must do in order to be a full member of society is to provide food for some female and her young."[15] For a 21st century individual who lives in a first world country, Mead's statement may be something belonging in a historical or an anthropological book, but for many people living in third world nations, this belief has been practiced for thousands of years and has never changed. In other words, we could say that some people live with the more modern belief that any person should be able to provide for himself and his offspring, whether male or female, while others persist in ancient, gender-biased beliefs and practices.

In the political arena, as presented in the Commission on the Status of Women, "In no country of the world has women's full "de jure" and "de facto" equality been achieved . . . Women are far from enjoying equal and full participation in political and public spheres."

Historically, the ideas and stereotypes about masculinity (strength) and femininity (weakness), have been reinforced and conceptualized by individuals such as Aristotle (trans. Peck), who from the roots of Western civilization, suggested: "The author of nature gave man strength of body and intrepidity of mind to enable him to face great hardships, and woman was given a weak and delicate constitution, accompanied by a natural softness and modest timidity, which fit her for sedentary life."[16]

These attributes of dominant (males) and submissive (females) have been universal throughout human history. It is only recently, by the accumulation of knowledge, that we have come to realize that no biological or psychological law of nature excludes females from being in charge. On the contrary, using history as a witness, we could argue that one of the biggest mistakes of humanity was in not realizing sooner the inability of most males to cooperate instead of compete, to help each other instead of fight, to build instead of destroy.

D'Andrade stated that the division of labor and roles directly related to primary and secondary gender characteristics and social organizations shows a degree of bias determined by sex. "In primitive societies, differentiation is essentially biological; the division of labor barely transcends the categories of age and sex, reproduction being the single most important biological factor in determining how men and women will live."[17]

The clash of civilizations is fueled by the ethnocentric attitude of most cultures, especially the more technologically advanced ones, which historically try to force their views of the world upon the less advanced and weaker cultures. The role of the woman may be the most important tradition that some of these cultures are trying to preserve. When it comes to the role of woman, we can see the reasons for conflicts, even within our modern technological American society; look at the philosophical gap between liberals and conservatives, or religious fanatics and secular intellectuals who cannot see eye to eye when it comes to the behavior and role of females.

To some of us, it seems logical and just that we should eliminate the most abusive practice in which many males engage—sexism. The sad reality is that in many different ways and many different degrees, sexism is alive and being practiced on a daily basis. In some parts of the world, it is as primitive and brutal as millennia ago. In other countries, such as the U.S., it is less severe and less tolerated but still present in almost every aspect of our lives (especially in government). Our society makes an effort to cover up the common stereotypes of woman as less able than man by using "politically correct" expressions and allowing a certain percentage of females to occupy positions of authority.

In a similar way, Boslooper and Hayes depicted the sex role differentiation as a psychological and biological stereotype: men's bodies are built up while women's are used. The female body is seen as a commodity, highly visible and salable in our commercial world, but a handicap in the world of sports. Most women get brainwashed into playing the "femininity game" and eventually see themselves the same way that men see them—as desirable objects with a built-in obsolescence.[18] It would be difficult to quantify the percentage of females that see themselves as objects, but the power of the media and the influence of pop culture are undeniable. The commercialization of the female body is still one of the most lucrative businesses in our society. As Bem describe it: "Either consciously or unconsciously, this sex-role division is part of the value system in which children soon learn that their mother is proud to be a moron when it comes to math and science, and that daddy is a little ashamed that he doesn't know all about these things."[19]

Many studies have tried to prove males' superior ability in some subjects, such as mathematics and science, but the evidence is inconclusive that a real difference exists between males and females and their intellectual capabilities. Until recently, biased socialization in most cultures has created psychological and institutional barriers in order to prevent females from having access to the same intellectual institutions and development that their male counterparts enjoy. However, in many parts of the world, education is finally allowing new generations the opportunity to drastically change the male-dominant paradigm into a more egalitarian one, where each individual realistically can achieve any goal that he or she wishes to achieve, regardless of his/her gender, race, or ethnicity.

Sherman and Beck have suggested that the "third world's" (less developed nations) pursuit of knowledge has been basically limited to a male activity since recorded history. Even though a few external barriers have been eliminated, sex-role expectations and social attitudes have remained the same, and generally serve to hinder women's progress.[20] The number one obstacle for equality among the genders is the lack of educational opportunities for millions of females. "A woman with a voice is, by definition, a strong woman. But the search to find that voice can be remarkably difficult. It's complicated by the fact that in most nations, women receive substantially less education than men."[21] Melinda Gates.

The old saying "knowledge is power" is exactly what many males do not want to share. In many societies, males know that when females acquire a good education, they will no longer tolerate the abuse and exploitation that they have been forced to endure out of the necessity of dependency on a male figure. In many cases, the fragile, primitive male ego is not ready for an intellectually equal or superior female partner. Since the beginning of time, his role has been one of dominance (by force), control, and power. In the words of Frieze and Ramsey, men display more dominance and high status cues than women, who are more gentle and warm in their nonverbal expressions. These behaviors are hard to change because of their unconscious nature, so they help to maintain the traditional sex roles.[22]

A number of authors describe the traditional sex roles in a simple but precise way. The personality of a young girl has been traditionally shaped, giving her a tendency to be dependent, passive, and conforming, as MacCoby and Jacklin[23] state. The very important fact that in most societies and cultures the female takes the family name of her husband when she gets married indicates the level of submission and, in many cases, the idea of belonging to a dominant male. Even in the popular language, we can see the connection between the female pronoun "she" and the concept of male ownership when referring to or naming possessions such as boats, motorcycles, and automobiles.

From a psychological point of view, the problem of sexism is even more complex to deal with because it is very difficult to achieve a high level of validity and reliability when studying human behavior that has been shaped and influenced so much by moral and cultural values.

In a more specific way, Kagan summarized sex roles:

> "Females are supposed to inhibit aggression and to inhibit open display of sexual urges. They are to be passive with men, to be nurturing, to cultivate attractiveness, and to maintain an emotionally-responsive, socially-poised, friendly posture with others. In contrast, males are to restrain their emotions in problem situations, be sexually aggressive, in control of regressive urges, and suppressive of strong emotions, especially anxiety."[24]

What portion of the male aggressive behavior is a product of nature or nurture we do not really know. What is clear is that in almost all societies throughout human history (and most likely pre-history), the physical and psychological requirement of being (or appearing to be) tough or in control has shaped the concept of masculinity. This aggressiveness, while practical and probably necessary many times in order to survive in the past, no longer is necessary. On the contrary, because of this aggressive attitude that most males still practice, we have many acts of violence at all levels—from individuals fighting in streets, bars, and schools to the unjustifiable wars among nations. The "bring it on" mentality, exemplified by former U.S. President George W. Bush, has been responsible for many deaths and economic hardships in both Iraq and the United States since the war began in 2003.

Another common stereotype concerning females which has prevented them from being elected to positions of power is the "time of the month" stereotype. Either explicitly or implicitly, a number of authors have presented discussions of presumed emotional fluctuations that occur throughout the menstrual cycle, i.e. "Women are subject to cyclic changes," or "The menstrual cycle imposes a rhythmic variability on the female of the species." These linguistic constructions, which attempt to describe psychological aspects of female's reproductive systems, imply that there are forces which are outside of their control, according to Parlee.[25] In addition, in the English language, as in most Indo-European ones, we can see gender bias in favor of males. For example, the adjective "virtuous" from the Latin "vir," meaning man, is a desirable attribute which implies a number of positive connotations, such as good, moral, honest, righteous, and worthy. On the other hand, the adjective "hysterical" from the Greek "hystera," meaning uterus, is used to describe negative, uncontrollable, and extremely emotional behavior attributed to females and has been used over and over by males to exclude females from positions of power.

The stereotype of women as socio-biologically handicapped individuals can be summarized in Western philosophy as follows: "Aristotle referred to women as 'misbegotten men'; Freud called them 'castrated'; Weiss has coined the term 'truncated men' to describe women who must be permitted to engage in sports."[26] The level of ignorance and prejudice that those stereotypes represent belong to the times when, for lack of knowledge and wisdom, man believed that the earth was the center of the solar system. Since the Copernican revolution, we no longer question the place of the earth in the heavens. It is also time that males recognize that they are not the center of our universe. In other words, there is no excuse for 21st century man to continue practicing the biggest discrimination of human history—sexism.

For many males, the idea of sharing power or being subordinated to females is difficult to deal with and accept. In most of the Western world, we have come a long way toward equality, but we still have a long way to go. According to Wolf and Filgsten, "White men had obtained power through their position in the work setting, while women's power traditionally had derived from their roles in the family. It has been argued that women gained social position from men in their lives, first from their fathers and then from their husbands." [27] Duberman hypothesized that from the little that is known about societies that existed before recorded time, most anthropologists have concluded that males, always and everywhere, have been the dominant beings on this planet. Two biological factors largely support this state of affairs: the male's superior strength, and the exclusive reproduction functions of the female.[28] According to these differences, it has been assumed that men and women may disagree on the characteristics of the ideal woman, but there has been general agreement that the main role of a woman has been to raise well-adjusted children. O'Barr attempted to explain the different specialization of the sexes by expressing it this way:

> "The ethnographic record does indeed suggest that physiological and anatomical differences between men and women are largely responsible for certain worldwide specialties: 1) In all hunting and gathering societies, men specialize in hunting large game, while women specialize in small game, shellfish, and vegetable products. 2) In all known human societies, men have exercised a dominate role in the maintenance of law and order in nondomestic contexts, especially in intergroup relations. 3) In all known societies, the primary police/military force consists of males, specially trained to use such weapons. 4) In all societies, women are the specialists in rearing infants." [29]

Psychologists and sociologists have tried to understand and explain human behavior and specific cultural and gender roles without arriving at clear conclusions. According to traditional psychoanalytic theory, competition and aggression are masculine traits.[30] Males are socialized to be "emotionally handicapped." Most males experience high levels of stress when their masculinity is challenged for a number of reasons, such as being perceived as too emotional, expressing fear, not being considered adequate in their sexual performance, and the list goes on and on to the point of creating a mal-adapted, insecure human with the need to prove to himself and others that he is a "real man." One can only speculate that individuals like Napoleon Bonaparte (with his "Napoleonic Complex") and Adolf Hitler (with his megalomaniacal and twisted view of the world) were just two insecure little men who had to prove their masculinity at all costs.

On the other hand, to rear a girl to conform to the stereotype of femininity was to rear her to be less aggressive, less physically strong, and less socially competent, according to the judgment of a group of experts. Here is the classic double bind presented to women: "Graphically stated, one can be feminine but incompetent or one can be competent but masculine."[31] We could argue from a psychological viewpoint that traditional stereotypes of masculinity and femininity are not healthy for either individuals or for society; they limit an individual's potential based upon gender and perpetuate the oppressive double standards.

Because of our modern, technologically-changing world, a growing body of literature has been dealing with the relatively new concept of psychological androgyny. Bem, Spence, and Singer suggested, "Androgyny refers to a specific way of joining the 'masculine' and 'feminine' aspects of a single human being."[32] The question is, in socializing both males and females, why not select the positive traits traditionally related to each gender and discourage the negative behaviors that harm individuals and society? Why not allow males to express and deal with their emotions in an open and healthy way? Why not emphasize cooperation instead of competition? The expressions "boys don't cry" or "take it like a man" had a purpose for a Spartan boy being trained to be a soldier in the past. Today, in the 21st century, males no longer need to be brainwashed into becoming fighting machines without the possibility of exploring and expressing their sensitive and emotional selves.

During the 2008 U.S. presidential campaign, the presidential candidate, Hillary Clinton, while answering a question posed by a woman in Portsmouth, NewHampshire, showed her emotions with a cracking voice and watery eyes. This may be one of the few moments when a politician actually presented a real concern for human beings, instead of acting as a calculating demagogue. Her answer was very real and showed the potential for positive change that could occur in the world if females were in charge of making political decisions that could improve society. In an emotional and sincere way, she answered a question about why she was seeking the presidency by saying, "This is very personal for me, not just political . . ." The same person who, as First Lady, tried so hard to provide health care for everyone summarized what leadership should be. With teary eyes she continued, "It's about our country. It's about our kids' futures. It's about all of us together." Unfortunately, in order to compete with the traditional, male political establishment, she then (as many other female candidates who have entered the political arena have had to do) had to become (or appear to be) aggressive and tough in an unreasonable way.

When combining biological (hormonal), psychological, and sociological factors, it is clear that it will take time for most males and societies to accept and adapt to a more "feminine male." Both historically and cross-culturally, masculinity and femininity have represented complementary domains of positive traits and behaviors. The author additionally observed that, "One emerges from a tour of the psychological literature on sex-roles with the distinct feeling that the world is composed of masculine males and feminine females, as well as sex-revered 'deviants.'" [33]

Unfortunately for humanity, historically speaking, male aggressive-dominated societies have not allowed less aggressive feminine or androgynous individuals to be in charge of governments and institutions. When males show sensitivity, love, and compassion, they are usually criticized for being weak or effeminate. The Machiavellian advice to political leaders (to be feared and not loved) in order to stay in power, exemplified the traditional male mentality, which may have been proper for a more "primitive" time period. However, for modern, democratic civilizations, equipped with nuclear weapons, this philosophy seems downright dangerous and usually results in conflict and human misery.

The concept of psychological androgyny implies that it is possible for an individual to be both masculine and feminine, depending on the situation and appropriateness of the moment. Eventually, it would be even more liberating if there were not any connotation of masculinity or femininity attached to any possible human behavior. For example, Jones observed,

> "The androgynous nature of all human beings is a biological fact that finds its counterpart in the realm of psychology. The psyche is bi-sexual, a fact that even Freud accepted under the advice of his doctor friend, Wilhelm Flies; the latter's research had convinced him that anatomically, embryologically, and chemically, human beings are normally bi-sexual."[34]

Without a universal and clear definition of what constitutes a "masculine" or a "feminine" attribute, we can only try to understand the social changes that we are experiencing in our modern world. The inter-relationship between biology, psychology, and culture is undeniable, especially when it comes to gender roles and social progress. According to Spance, et. al., androgyny is defined, not as a balance of masculinity and femininity, but instead, as the possession of a high degree of both characteristics.[35] For many years American society has considered masculinity to be the sign of a psychologically healthy male. It was assumed that "the values of the Masculine Mystique in this country emerged from our early agrarian society which tamed the wilderness and started the American experiment in Democracy."[36] For new generations, the gap between the genders is definitely smaller than for our predecessors, but consciously or subconsciously, different gender roles and expectations still play a role in our contemporary, everyday lives.

Goffman suggested that, in our society, when a man and a woman cooperate in a face to face project, the man, it would seem, is probably going to perform the executive role, if one can be fashioned.[37] In many ways, just as racism still exists, sexism is part of the idiosyncratic behavior of many members of our society. From sexist humor to lower pay for women to glass ceilings, society (if not out in the open, then behind closed doors) still believes that, for the most part, males should be in charge. This is an especially prevalent belief among males.

Hart wrote critically about sex-roles saying, "American society cuts the penis off the male who enters dance, and places it on the woman who participates in competitive athletics."[38] Many occupations clearly reflect the expectations for the genders. The stereotype of male dancers or hairdressers as being gay or effeminate is a common one. The disproportionate amount of money and effort put into male athletic programs, versus female ones, is one of the many areas in which society demonstrates that the fight for equality and fairness is far from over.

In a similar way, "A number of studies suggest that women have less territory and take up less physical space than men. This smaller space for women is more frequently violated than for that of men."[39] The assumption that females need less space or resources is founded in the historically-limiting role that females have been allowed to play in society. The characteristically male (macho) mentality of territorial and mate possession can be observed in the animal kingdom, in which the male of the species must fight competitors for possession of both his territory and his females, clearly marking both in some way.

According to Block, parents, perhaps particularly fathers, emphasize different values in raising their sons and daughters.[40] American culture's emphasis on masculine machismo and feminine passivity seems to be impeding the development of mature ego functioning. Today, however, mainly through education, gender roles and opportunities have increased, especially for women. Females are slowly beginning to gain ground in different occupations and even in politics, frequently against the will of the "good old boys," however.

Several researchers have attempted to describe these changes that have affected American society. As Ridley states, "In the 20th century, increased life expectancy, reduction in fertility, and increasing migration within and between societies continue to change the patterns of women's lives and relations within marriage and the family."[41] The drastic changes in the concept of marriage itself in present day America is another important factor to take into consideration when referring to the ever-changing society. With a divorce rate close to 50% and new forms of marital arrangements, we are witnessing the clash between traditional marriage and new concepts, such as gay marriage, in which the individual's rights are put to the test in our democratic experiment.

The traditional male identity is being challenged to the point that homophobia is becoming politicized and, sadly, used by religious leaders to claim moral superiority. Honest and rational education could allow our society to understand and accept human nature with dignity and tolerance. In a few words, many people confuse what is "normal" with what is "natural" and believe that homosexuality is unnatural and, therefore, immoral or against God's design. If we clarify, that "normal" is what a particular society at a particular point in its history considers to be the norm, and that "natural" is what happens in nature (not something artificially created by man), we can conclude that in our society homosexuality may not be "normal," yet, it is "natural" because it happens in nature. Contrary to some ignorant views, homosexuality is not learned. The best way to understand that human sexual attraction is simply natural is by honestly asking yourself if you have a choice (regardless of your sexual orientation) about what particular individual you are physically (sexually) attracted to. No one can teach or convince another person to be attracted to someone if this attraction does not exist. It has to come from within the individual. To test this idea, try to physically like or be attracted to someone that you find ugly or unattractive. You cannot choose; it is a bio-chemical reaction that causes you to like someone, whether that person is skinny, fat, blonde, brunet, male, female, or any other set of attributes. The homophobic, sexist, and fragile male ego refuses to understand and accept common sense, logic, and positive humanistic progress.

Spence & Helmrich additionally observed that in the United States, both evolutionary and revolutionary changes in sexual differentiations have taken place during the last 150 years. Changes in social attitudes and practices have most visibly been in the form of gender role broadening and greater permissiveness for women and have centered particularly on our conceptions of the "traditional" family and women's amount of participation in the labor force.[42]

The industrial revolution had indeed been accompanied by a trend toward the development of greater similarity in the social roles of males and females. Likewise, the technological advances of the last few decades have created the proper conditions for the elimination of sexism. As Hersh suggested, the growth of industrialization has played a major role in the development of a feminist leadership. Burgeoning factories took over much of the work previously done at home, lightening housewives' burdens. Industrialization also created job opportunities which caused widespread migrations from the farm to the city and attracted a great number of immigrants. These developments then helped to give women a cheap source of domestic help. This combination of circumstances provided the urban, middle-class woman with more leisure time to carry on reform activities.[43]

Lederer assumed that the change of our basic conception of sex-roles was due to the fact that "Many of the important roles in our society are dependent upon intelligence, the ability to work for or with other people, or the power to utilize certain specialized knowledge, like mathematics or physics; these are capabilities which both men and women possess. Therefore, role distinctions are being made less on a sexual than a functional basis."[44]

The sexist argument that males must be better at certain things and more intelligent than females has been the justification to exclude women from the acquisition of power and knowledge. The illogical explanation of trying to prove male superiority by comparing the number of political and religious male leaders, scientists, and philosophers who exist in society (as opposed to the number of females in such positions) would only make sense if, historically, both males and females were always provided the same opportunities to excel. The reality is that not only were females not permitted to obtain an education and to achieve leadership positions, but they were also socialized to accept their submissive roles as part of the natural order. How absurd it is to pretend that more males achieved more things based on their superiority, rather than pointing to the real cause for the difference—deprivation of education and opportunities for females. There is no way to know what females could have achieved, had males not denied them the same opportunities given to men. However, even though females are still struggling with all kinds of barriers (especially psychological ones), the real potential and capabilities of women are beginning to reveal themselves in some of the developed nations. Sadly, however, it is still a reality in many countries of the world that social and psychological barriers for women, resulting in gender inequality, are still as strong today as they were centuries ago.

"The world has never yet seen a truly great and virtuous nation because in the degradation of woman, the very fountains of life are poisoned at their source." Lucretia Mott[45]

Another aspect of society which reveals gender biases is that of language connotations. We cannot divorce language from culture. Therefore, by analyzing some of the meanings of words used to describe both males and females, we can see the linguistic, sexist world that we inherit. Using the Spanish language as an example, we can clearly see the double standards and connotative implications in the following words:

Zorro (male fox) = wise, agile

Zorra (female fox) = prostitute

Perro (male dog) = man's best friend

Perra (female dog) = bitch, prostitute

Aventurero (male adventurer) = valiant, intrepid

Aventurera (female adventurer) = prostitute, "gold-digger"

Hombre publico (public man) = personality, public official

Mujer publica (public woman) = prostitute

Atrevido (male) = brave, daring

Atrevida (female) = insolent, a woman with bad manners

Soltero (unmarried man) = desirable, intelligent

Soltera (unmarried woman) = pitiful old maid

Machista (male) = manly man

Femenista (female) = Lesbian, militant woman

Suegro (male) = father in-law

Suegra (female) = witch

In other words, the terms that describe men always have positive connotations, while the exact same terms used for females have negative connotations. Certainly, sexism is alive and well in language choices. John Driessnack further contributes to this observation by stating, "Women, for example, are often the scapegoats for male lust. Phrases such as, 'She was asking for it,' and 'Well, look at how she was dressed,' make this point clear and obvious."[46] This is only a small sample, among many other words and expressions, that exemplify the culturally-imbedded ideas and stereotypes that are part of everyday life in the majority of cultures throughout the world. In theory, we live in a non-prejudiced society, but in reality, we still live with the primitive sense of inequality.

The same criticism has been raised concerning the "real" possibilities for the emancipation of women. As O'Neil & Blake suggested, experience has demonstrated that formal barriers to women's emancipation, such as not being able to vote, fewer educational opportunities, job discrimination, and the like, are not as serious and are more susceptible to change than are the domestic, institutional, and social customs that tend to keep women at home.[47]

The reduction in the number of children that modern couples produce in developed nations, paired with an older age when they choose to start a family, are fundamental factors that allow females to participate in areas and professions that were off limits to them in the past. Family planning and education are two of the most important tools that women have in order to break free from the limiting roles of females as just mothers and housewives.

As a complementary argument in favor of the significant change in the traditional sex-roles in the Unites States:

> "The urban sector offered women both increased autonomy within the traditional sphere of the home and an extension of their activities into the 'outside' world. No longer were the home and its functions deemed to be the sole proper focus of activity for women. Indeed, what was considered to be women's proper sphere underwent considerable expansion during the era of Women's Liberation."[48]

Now that we have experienced some change in our society toward equality among the genders, we can be optimistic about the potential benefit that it will bring to all of us when females start to use their nurturing, positive influence in the decision-making process at both national and international levels. In a similar way, Bullough suggested that

> "Part of the change was due to the fact that Americans were increasingly urbanized, and the home was no longer the all-consuming job it had been, especially when children entered school, and the technological developments of the twentieth century made housekeeping a part-time job. This, in turn, meant that women had more freedom to enter the job market. Though discrimination continued to exist, the barriers were psychological rather than legal."[49]

Education is the best way to end the psychological and cultural barriers that continue to prevent women from taking control of positions of power and leadership. Less than 15% of leadership positions are held by females worldwide. The highest percentage of female leadership positions are held by women in the Scandinavian countries, which also have the highest standards of living and the lowest crime rates.

Sex Roles in Third-World Countries: The Past Meets the Future

In order to understand and compare the roles of male and female stereotypes in third world countries, especially in Latin America, we need to be aware that many people in developing nations live in the 21st century (mainly in the large modern cities), while other people live in the past (mainly in the countryside and small towns). As has happened in the United States, there have been some positive changes made in order to reduce sexism in these developing countries. However, for the most part, stereotypical roles for men and women continue to be the mainstream societal practice, imposed by the traditional male-dominated cultures of these countries.

Stevens suggested that life for the Latin American man, with regards to the role of "machismo," means being forced to be aggressive at all times, with the only safe outlet for aggression being the woman.[50] Having many children and his wife's perpetual pregnancy are treated as visible proof of the man's virility. Men have the power, while women have the love, and there is very little room for change. An additional burden for women in the Latin culture is that they are considered as images of the Virgin Mary, which means that they should conduct themselves in a "pure" manner at all times. They are also the central figures of the home and family, having to constantly strive to maintain a harmonious environment and to rear perfect children. Yet, they have been traditionally considered innately inferior and subordinate to men. The variations in this sex role stereotype occur in every Latin American country, varying only slightly according to social class and various other cultural factors. Studies have shown that among the urban, middle class, increasing industrialization, better education, and family planning are slowly changing the inferior status of women.[51]

Despite some minor changes in Latin cultural practices, Sau says the portrayal of the macho role is used to depict the amorous impulses and sexual potential of the male, whereas, for females, the maternal role is culturally emphasized.[52] Rueather hypothesized about the dualistic images of women; women are seen as being both inferior and superior to men. The monotheistic religions have developed two major images of females: the sinful Eve and the saintly Mary. The carnal, temptation-prone woman juxtaposed with the maternal, nurturing, good mother are the two images that women have been tagged with since the beginning of time.[53]

Traditionally, men are viewed in many cultures as being more violent and hostile than women, who are expected to behave passively, obediently, and submissively in order to complement and counteract men's nature.[54]

As a result of all this gender stereotyping, remarkable differences exist between the behavior of males and females in Latin American countries, for the most part. Characteristics of male behavior in Latin America, as defined by the concept of "machismo," are considered opposite to the gender role defined by the Spanish word describing a female's behavior as feminine. Aggressiveness, sexual urges, feelings of superiority, and demanding respect from others are clearly male attributes. Contrastingly, the characteristics and expectations of the female gender role are those of sweetness, submissiveness, lack of sexual interest, pre-marital virginity, and maternity. Traditional roles are well accepted in Latin America; women are revered as images of the Virgin Mary and as central figures of the home and family. Yet they have been traditionally considered innately inferior and subordinate to males.[55]

Another example of the influence of culture in Latin America and traditional societies is exemplified in the famous play, *Yerma,* by the author Garcia Lorca.[56] His play depicts sterility as a woman's greatest possible tragedy in life. The inability to have children in societies where the main, and sometimes only, purpose in life for a female is to be a mother and raise children, is tragic. Sterility is taken to the extreme by institutions like the Catholic Church, which allows divorce or annulment of a marriage only when the couple cannot have children.

Since the majority of Latin Americans are Roman Catholics, the message of who should be in charge of the family and society is clearly stated and represented. From the Pope on down to priests, a lack of female representation in church hierarchy clearly portrays the female role as a very subordinate position. The tremendous power conveyed by the fact that "spiritual leaders" can only be males is enough to create a psychological barrier that will maintain the status quo of a sexist society for some time to come. When, and if, the Church (like many other religious institutions) ever realizes that the male authoritarian structure does not equate with the basic principles of fairness and love, perhaps it will cease to be so hypocritical. From a spiritual point of view, no gender should have a monopoly on who is in charge of representing God on Earth.

Even though there has been some change in sex roles in modern times, in order for sexual equality to become a reality, there must be, not only a change in the value system to provide the ideological preconditions, but technological, economical, and political factors to support such changes. By educating our children and practicing what we preach (equality, justice, fairness, tolerance) we could begin to see some of the changes that we pretend that we have accomplished, not only in quantity but also in quality.

Cross-Cultural Studies Related to Gender Roles:

The cross-cultural mode in interpersonal behavior has been categorized in a relatively similar way by several authors. According to D'Andrade, males are generally more sexually active, more dominant, more deferred to, more aggressive, less responsible, less nurturing, and less emotionally expressive than females. However, the author explained that the degree to which these differences can be observed varies, according to the culture in which a male is reared. Maleness and femaleness are institutionalized as statuses in every culture and become psychological identities for most of the individuals in the culture.[57] In general, the subordinated and passive condition of women can be exemplified by a cross-cultural analysis in which Bullough observed:

> "Whether these Eastern women were any worse off than Western women at comparable stages in development, however, is debatable. Although foot binding seems a particularly cruel form of confinement, in many ways, it was not any more debilitating than the attempts of Western women to narrow their waistlines to eighteen or twenty inches [with a corset], and it had the same effect of limiting women's physical activity."[58]

From a realistic and a historical perspective, it is impossible to pretend to change the traditional and cultural values of developing countries by imposing our modern, Western culture on the rest of the world. In reality, we, (the so-called modern, civilized society) live in the 21st century, while many people in different regions of the world live in the past. However, even modern societies are not completely ready to change all of our cultural practices and values in order to adopt a more egalitarian way of life. Furthermore, we can begin to understand why cultures, such as those in the Islamic Middle East, may reject our Western cultural values if we try to imagine how difficult it would have been to make our great-grand parents accept and allow the sexual behavior, fashions, and morality of our modern times. A century ago, the great majority of people in our Western cultures would not have allowed their daughters to dress in the revealing, "immoral" fashions of today. We should ask ourselves what our great-grandparents would have done had a more powerful and influential culture tried to impose their "immoral" practices upon them. If an average parent of 1800's American society saw the way that our present day youth dance, talk, dress, and express their sexuality, they most likely would not only reject it but would find ways to protect their traditional way of life from it. Even in today's society, we will find many Americans who are very concerned about the direction that our society is taking. Ironically, some of the extremist religious and political leaders in our country would be on the same side as the Muslin extremists in trying to forbid and punish the more open and liberal behavior and views of the "progressive," Western civilization.

In a cross-cultural study of gender differences in socialization, Barry, Bacon, and Child found that among 110 cultures surveyed, 82% expected boys to be more self-reliant than girls.[59] The universal division of roles according to gender has been assumed by individuals like Goldberg. According to this author, cross-cultural compilations of ethnographical materials show the universality of male dominance with the same certainty that they demonstrate patriarchy.[60] The extreme of this male dominance could be sadly illustrated by the picture on the cover of *Time* magazine (January,27,2010) of "A'isha, a shy, 18-year-old, Afghan woman who was sentenced by a Taliban commander to have her nose and ears cut off for fleeing her abusive in-laws."[61]

The concept of patriarchy (male-dominated society) is evident in every aspect of life. From the expression "The head of the family" to "Who wears the pants?" the implication is that males are in charge. Most leadership positions in most significant areas of human endeavor are held and controlled by males. From presidents of nations to religious leaders to chancellors of universities, the overwhelming majority of leaders has been, and still is, men.

On the other hand, Maccoby has suggested that if we reverse the roles for the responsibility of child training for males and females, we might still discover that females feel a need to be responsible for child training, and males don't feel the same need.[62] The traditional view of females as being "naturally designed" to take care of children is a universal one. The fact that breast feeding can only be performed by females somewhat justifies this concept of gender roles when it comes to child rearing. It is undeniable that most females provide a very warm, caring, and nurturing feeling to their offspring. However, that observation does not exclude males from playing a very important role in the care and nurturing of their children. Today, with the technology we have to pump and refrigerate breast milk or simply to buy infant formula, females, as well as males, can provide the proper nutrition and satisfy the basic needs of children.

In contrast to those ideas, Orr wrote that "Any statement about the sexual role of women in history should be made in the context of race, class, and economic position within a given culture or subculture and within a given historical era."[63] The never-ending argument of nature versus nurture will probably continue to be debated for some time. Regardless of which one has more influence on our behavior, however, the fact is that either because of biology or psychology, males are overwhelmingly more aggressive and less nurturing than females. Even in Western cultures, men have always dominated women. The "real" man was the individual who could use heavy tools, hunt food for his family, and fight off enemies. Physical strength, having been the basis for survival, helped place men in positions of power, allowing them to make the rules and the decisions.

However, as Radford suggested, the physical advantages that men had over women in primitive times in the struggle for survival may have become obsolete with the development of modern civilization. Mechanization and power tools have replaced the need for and use of human physical power. We now have machines that are able to be used by any individual, regardless of their gender. The only requirement for the use of these machines is training and mental abilities. Modern firearms can neutralize the strongest man on the planet with a single bullet. A remote control drone plane can destroy a building from thousands of miles away. Real power is no longer muscle power, but rather brain power. We have come to the point in our civilization which requires us to use our brains before we let our aggressive hormones dictate our behaviors.[64]

Some researchers have attempted to support the hypothesis that the changes in traditional sex roles have been initiated by advanced technology in more modern societies. As DeReincourt suggested, a new historical development, by definition, is initiated by those societies that are the most progressive in their times.[65] Quiet logically, it was mainly in the English-speaking (and to a smaller extent the Scandinavian Countries) where feminine consciousness-raising first began to manifest itself. According to Giele, the patriarchal practices of the typical peasant family in developing countries is the main element that creates obstacles to women's freedom in those countries. The author also suggested that now that modernization is proceeding somewhat faster in developed countries, such as France, the United States, and Japan, the dichotomy between home life and work is being separated into a still larger variety of possible options for both men and women. On the governmental services side, many public services are becoming available in all modern societies. They have expanded health care, pension plans, child care options, and social security. All of these services help to relieve the family of its gender-driven functions. In the process, the woman's primary role as family nurturer is lessened, and the man's role as the primary bread winner is also being reduced. At the same time, women's options outside the home in education, employment, and political and cultural expression are widening even further.[66]

From the traditional male's point of view, it easy to understand his anxiety and level of rejection produced by such changes. The idea of sharing power and control is not an easy one to accept, especially when it is imposed by cultural and ideological beliefs. After the industrial revolution, a man's worth was measured in terms of his technical skills and intellectual productiveness, as shown by the amount of money he made. As the twentieth century progressed, women were able to develop many of the same skills as men had acquired, as well as intellectual prowess. They also started gaining employment parity with men and earning almost as much money in certain fields. However, it is important to note that even though in Western, modern societies there is a certain level of equality among the genders, females are still being underpaid by approximately thirty percent, especially in managerial positions. Once again, the male's obsession with control and power does not allow common sense and fairness to prevail.

Despite these advances in the workplace, women are still at a physical disadvantage in male-dominated cultures. Bullough made astute observations regarding the disadvantages of child bearing and rearing, even in modern cultures. As he stated,

> "In the early development of society, physical strength was a significant variable in helping to establish the subordinate position of women. The greater size and strength of the male made him better able than the female to fight off animals and human enemies, and even though the female in individual cases might have been equal to the male in strength, as a group they were not. In return for male protection, women offered obedience. Civilization progressed, and physical strength became less important. However, women were still somewhat handicapped by their greatest disadvantage until fairly recently—fertility."[67]

Recently, some authors have indicated that the development of birth control methods has theoretically eliminated the biological inevitability of motherhood. According to this phenomenon, "Women can plan if and when they wish to have children"[68] However, it is one thing to say what we can or cannot do, or what we want to do or do not want to do; it is quite another to say that we must live with the socialized expectations of our families, friends, and society. In first world countries, the choice of a female to become a mother or not is becoming more and more acceptable. But in third world countries, the principal role of a woman is still to bear and rear children. The phenomenon of social change has been discussed by many in the last few decades; indeed, anthropologist Margaret Mead has pointed out that we may already be moving toward a system under which, as she puts it, "Parenthood would be limited to a small number of families whose principal function would be child rearing, leaving the rest of the population free to function, for the first time in history, as individuals."[69]

Some of the conflicts that we currently experience on this planet, especially in the Middle East, are directly related to the cultural confrontation between the traditional, male-oriented societies and the liberal, Western ones. It may be, as O'Neil has suggested, that "Many men have typically been socialized to believe that:

a) men are superior to women in nearly every area of life
b) women are to be dominated, protected, and subordinated
c) men are to set and enforce the daily norms, values, and expectations
d) men are to work in the "real" world and women in the home
e) men are to use their power, control, and aggressiveness to make most of the decisions[70]

These values may have been functional in a non-industrialized, frontier society, but they are dysfunctional in today's technological, computerized society"

The problem is that we live in a world in which the modern/ technological and the traditional/ agricultural societies co-exist in a very shrinking world. Change is coming too fast for some people to deal with in a peaceful and reasonable way; instead, they are using whatever means they have at their disposal to protect their way of life. We can only speculate on the percentage of males, and even females, who do believe that males are superior in many ways and, therefore, should be in control. Because of so-called "political correctness," many people refuse to express their honest opinions and beliefs on this matter and will give false answers, if pressed for a statement. Within the comfort and acceptance of their own groups, many individuals who publically claim that we are equal, would reveal their true sexist and racist views. Only with time and thoughtful education will we one day achieve real equality.

Theorists have begun to question the traditional roles of philosophy related to sex issues. As Chasteen postulates, man has been limited for most of his existence to a view of sex as being only for procreation. It is not really the act of sexual intercourse that lay behind all the prohibitions against it, but the likelihood of conception. Over the last century or two, Western man has more and more intervened in his own evolution. Many of the operations of nature have been described and modified as advancing technology is applied to them, as has been the case with sex. Contraceptive technology has made it possible to separate the act of sexual intercourse from actual conception, making it possible (and necessary) for us to rethink the philosophy of sex, which was worked out before contraception existed. A very simple formula can be stated:

Coitus - contraception = procreation

Coitus + contraception = expression[71]

The complexity of human sexuality is one of the areas in which male-dominated societies have tried to emphasize the difference between males and females. Without any scientific evidence or possibility to detectibly measure the physiological differences between male and female sexual "desires" or "needs," societies have fabricated the myth of male sexual needs to justify historically very promiscuous behavior in men. On the other hand, female sexuality has been limited and controlled by trying to shape (in a very puritanical way) sexual relations as only for procreational purposes. The recently-publicized death penalty sentence of an Iranian woman for the "crime" of adultery is representative of the extremes that male-dominated cultures are willing to take to deny females of their human sexuality.

According to the British Broadcast Corporation (BBC), "Under Iran's strict interpretation of Islamic law, sex before marriage (fornication) is punishable by 100 lashes, but married offenders (adulterers) are sentenced to death by stoning. The stones used must be large enough to cause the condemned person much pain, but not sufficient to kill him immediately." Social and cultural stereotypes are responsible for the continuation of the double standards that most societies practice today, and only through education will we be able to move forward to a more egalitarian society.

In a similar way, one conclusion to be drawn from these observations is that the male's superior strength has conferred an adaptation upon socio-cultural systems that has made the control and use of weapons and instruments of the hunt and warfare a male specialty. This conclusion must not be confused with the popular notion that it is "natural" for men to be the warriors and hunters, or that it is "natural" for women to cook and take care of children. O'Barr states:

> "Modern anthropology has conclusively demonstrated that there is nothing purely "natural" about human hunting, warfare, political organization, or domestic life. All socio-cultural practices represent the selective result of the interaction between culture and nature" [72]

The author also suggested that in advanced, industrial contexts, the physiological and anatomical differences between males and females no longer decisively influence manipulation of the instruments of production of political-military control: "Modern weaponry and industrial automation cancel out the physiological and anatomical basis of male supremacy." He additionally observed that with the long-range trend toward decreased fertility under industrial conditions, "Women are pregnant, on average, less than three percent of their lives. Furthermore, bottle formulas have eliminated or greatly reduced the period of biologically unavoidable breast feeding". The author concludes by saying:

"No single explanation satisfactorily accounts for the revolution of women's status cross-culturally. The important point in all the explanations is that the allocation of roles and the subsequent asymmetry have been tied in some way to the child-bearing activities of women and the ecological requirements for existence. As women are freed from an inevitable tie to pregnancy and lactation, and as societal requirements for the physical strength are made obsolete by technology, the basis for sexual asymmetry becomes questionable." [73]

The change produced by industrialization has been assessed by the United Nations Data and National Census Data for 37 countries which provided the basis for this analytical impact of demographic factors on women's roles and status. As expected, of the three groups of countries—high natality and mortality; high natality and low mortality; and low natality and mortality—the third group had the highest female economic participation rates. It is suggested that the increasing age at marriage and proportion of single women now found in some developing countries, as well as other demographically-induced social changes, will produce the educational and occupational advances and equalitarian marital roles found in industrialized countries.[74]

As technology and medical advances become more available to more people throughout the world, infant mortality becomes less of a factor in developing nations for families to want to have many children. By having fewer children, females could realistically begin to play more flexible and diversified roles, including participating in practically all professions and occupations. Problems arise in developing countries, however, when life-saving medical care, coupled with a lack of education and reliable birth control, results in a drastic increase in birth rate in our already overpopulated world. It is imperative that the world community synchronize the technological changes with education at a global level. International responsible and moral leadership is what the human race is hungry for. With the participation of the modern (liberated) woman in leadership positions, it is possible that a new and improved civilization can develop.

A growing body of literature indicates that if man's asserted superiority to woman is attributable merely to brute strength, it would seem logical that as civilization evolved, and as physical strength became less necessary for survival, the position of women should have improved. Nevertheless, the nature of our reproductive processes, along with the responsibilities of caring for the young, still manages to keep women at a disadvantage in the working world, and it is this factor, rather than the home and family, that has carried the highest status in most societies. So in other words, women's greatest disadvantage, until just recently, has been their unlimited fertility.[75]

According to this hypothesis, William and Jackson observed that:

> "The modern woman in the first half of the twentieth century desired equality in every way, beginning with sex and the vote. At about the same time, contraceptive devices were perfected. Now woman could be man's equal, not only in society, in business, and in scholarship, but also in sexual convenience; the sex act could be enjoyed by both without the woman's having to fear an unwanted pregnancy".[76]

More importantly, for the first time in human history, women could become the architects of our political, economic, and social systems, which most likely will be a tremendous improvement over the conflictive unfair world so far created by man. As a consequence of these fundamental changes, it is quite clear that a major factor which made men examine and change their sex role are the dramatic recent changes in women's own definitions of themselves and what they see as their roles in society.[77]

The effects of change in values became part of the change in sex roles, thus affecting the value of conceiving children. Demographers have described what they call a demographic transition—the fall in Europe's fertility rate with the spread of industrialization and economic development. One way of explaining this pattern would be that as industrialization and urbanization increased, the perceived cost of children—psychologically, socially, and economically—became obviously clear to both men and women.[78]

The change in gender roles from the traditional, agrarian society to the modern, technological one is clearly explained by the following factors:

1. For the traditional agricultural society, where more than 90% of the population worked planting and harvesting crops, the more children a family produced, the more laborers there were to work on the farm, and the more product and profit the family derived.
2. For the modern, industrial society, there is no need to have a large family, since most people are no longer employed in the agricultural sector. Therefore, fewer children are actually a benefit to families, since a majority of women are now employed and cannot stay home to raise a large family. Add to that the high cost of raising children and a smaller living space in urban and suburban regions, and the reasons for the declining fertility rate among industrial societies is obvious.

Several researchers have demonstrated that research on the causes and effects of the changing value of children is, therefore, crucial to understanding change in sex-typed behavior (Bernard,[79] ; Hoffman,[80] ; Veevers,[81]). The impact of cultural change negating the necessity of having a large nuclear family has created the opportunity for a real change in gender roles. By having only one or two children at the most, modern women can afford to obtain an education and a career, thus making her more competitive in the work force and liberating her from male dominance.

Recently, theorists have begun to suggest that previous sex-role stereotypes and practices have been shaken up to prepare for the changes technology was producing then and continues to produce today.[82] The effects of technological development on sex-roles are being observed to different degrees in most of the world. Some countries, like Denmark and Sweden, have welcomed this change with open arms and have achieved more equality among the genders than any other society on earth. Some other countries have refused to allow gender role changes to be part of their so-called development efforts. The feminist movement that started centuries ago was not able to really transform society until the middle of the 20th century when, finally, with the help of improved education and reliable birth control methods, females began to take their place in society as men's equals. As Lynn has said, "If there had been no feminist movement to perform this function, one would have had to be invented."[83] In other words, "It is required to help us to see what is actually happening in our society today and to redefine sex roles to meet these new conditions. Changing sex-specialized norms and sex-typed behavior is not a take-it-or-leave-it option. It is a fundamental imperative. The question is not whether to do it but rather how to do it."[84]

We should also inquire as to when this change will fully be implemented everywhere. For some, like the Taliban, who operate in Afghanistan, it may take more than one generation to understand that equality among genders should not have to be incompatible with their spiritual and conservative views but, instead, could be a positive step toward a more just and healthy society.

The modern woman is not the promiscuous and superficial one portrayed in many Hollywood movies. On the contrary, the majority of modern females not only manage to take care of their homes and families but also have second jobs in almost all of the occupations and areas of life.

The materialistic culture, which emerged as a result of the industrial era, is the first step which permits women to have independent jobs and to control the money they earn (a fact which greatly improves their bargaining position within the family) and to assert their rights and wishes within that group. By using basic math (the more power females have, the less power the males have), we can see how many males are reluctant to accept the change in gender roles. The traditional economic dependency of females on males is no longer a powerful factor to keep women (especially in developed nations) subjugated by men and treated as second class citizens. On the other hand, it has also made men realize that they can more easily end difficult relationships and walk away from women who would previously have been economically dependent upon them.

In a comprehensive study on this demographic change and women's roles and status, Ridley pointed out what happened to women's roles as industrialization proceeded in Western societies. A smaller proportion of women's lives were being devoted to the bearing and rearing of children. The decline in the mortality rate contributed to a surplus of women in the marriageable age group. Thus, a demographic surplus of females resulted in a larger proportion of single women than had been the case in previous generations. The larger the number of women remaining single, and the diminishing importance of the reproductive role, the greater the economic participation of women in society.[85]

On the other hand, in many developing nations, lack of education (paired with social expectations placed upon females) limits their ability to be financially independent and to participate in the political and economic arena—in other words, to have any power. Bernard found an inverse relationship between fertility rate and the proportion of all advanced degrees earned by women.[86]

Even though motherhood may be the most powerful and important concept of all for humans, it does not have to exclude women from being in charge of so many other aspects of living in a civilized world. On the contrary, because females experience the biological and psychological phenomenon of a nine-month gestation period and then give birth to another human being, women have a very special bond (motherhood) with their children that no male will ever have. It is because of this special bond with other human beings and the desire to protect and nurture them that we can speculate and suggest that if more females were in charge as political leaders, the historically male way to deal with others by force (war) could be greatly reduced and eventually eliminated. By using education and seriously practicing the democratic principles, we could let the informed people decide what kind of leaders and political systems they want to have and the kind of society in which they want to live.

The universal relationship between biological make-up and human behavior appear to be in a process of transformation from biological determinism of sex-roles to intellectual and psychological determinism. The need for adaptation to a highly technological society has produced a conflictive stage in the process of social evolution, in which our traditional concepts of family, marriage, and sex-roles are being challenged. As Lederer states, "We cannot return to the simple life of an agricultural or primitive community in this atomic, industrial age; we must modify our outmoded attitudes, beliefs, and institutions to accommodate current social realities."[87] The phenomena of overpopulation and industrialization have had tremendous impacts on social development. As a result, a growing trend toward the understanding of world community and interaction among its members has become imperative.

We can perceive a greater change in the roles that females play in society because there are an infinite number of attitudes and roles that the females can change. The world outside of the home, especially in this highly technological and industrialized society, has opened the door for new behavioral patterns and roles for females. On the other hand, there is less room for males to be able to improve or expand their occupational roles. Sex roles at this point in the social evolution are much less shaped by traditional ideology than by the modern, mobile, and transitory society. They are not only strongly influenced by social, economic, and political factors, but are also manifested in a breaking away from biological determiners. Therefore, the choice of sex roles involves taking a rational position based in value hierarchy, relevant consideration of circumstantial facts, and individual experiences and judgment. So whether or not particular behaviors are appropriate depends primarily upon the particular values and the specific situations for each individual.

Analyzing countries from a historical continuum shows that we can equate the differences of socio-economic and technological levels of each one of them, with the values, opportunities, and circumstances that probably influence their practiced sex roles and behavioral types. Progressive differences in percentages of individuals falling into the androgynous category shows the United States as being one of the highest in technological and economic development, and also one with the highest in the number of individuals identified as androgynous. This relationship can be explained from a historical perspective by analyzing the evolution of sex roles based on assumptions and anthropological records.

The fact that, historically, double standards were and still are common in most societies, raises the questions of why, when, where and how we developed and continue to maintain the traditional concepts of male dominance over females? To answer this question, we can use some chronological speculations to connect the past with the present and to see the direction of sex roles in the future.

According to pre-historic records and observations of the majority of "primitive" people that live in modern times, it is possible to observe a clear division of labor and roles between the genders. It is clear and easy to accept the concept of maternity as a universal phenomenon throughout the history of the human race. But it is not as clear, and there is not real evidence, that indicates that the concept of paternity has always existed. If we look at most mammals, it would be difficult to identify the exclusive role of the male as the father of a newborn. In the case of humans, it is possible to consider that for pre-historic man, who had very little knowledge of human physiology, had a completely different concept of time, and enjoyed a much shorter life span compared to modern man, the relationship between sexual intercourse and paternity was not always clear. During this time of pre-history, it can be assumed that the division of labor and roles were basically related to the physical abilities of individuals. Since females could get pregnant most of their lives and had a weaker physical constitution than males, the asymmetrical roles were functional for survival and adaptation to the environment.

If these assumptions are right, probably the next significant step of the socio-evolutionary process of sex roles was the learning of physiological relationships between sexual intercourse and paternity. From this point, it is possible to understand why the institution of marriage was created and to see the socio-biological origin of traditional sex roles. From the creation of the practice of marriage also emerges the creation of some of the strongest double standards between the genders. This phenomenon can be explained by assuming that when man began to use and shape the concept of paternity (which implies responsibility towards his children), he probably asked woman for virginity and/or fidelity as a biological guarantee of his participation in the creation of their children. Around these two rules, especially around fidelity, is where many of the other double standards came about. The limitations and restrictions that traditionally were part of the woman's life have been designed to keep females out of the genetic pool that represent most environments outside of the home. This hypothesis combines with the fact of a long gestation period and, in general, physical differences between females and males that can account for some explanation of our traditional sex roles.

One could argue that one of the main components in the clash of civilizations between Western Civilization and the Islamic World has its roots in the role of the female and the traditional protection of the fragile and insecure concept of paternity. History is full of abuses, murders, and injustices committed against women in the name of honor and morality. Religions have, in many ways, perpetuated the idea that the role of females should be limited and subordinated to males. As most individuals or groups who hold power, males are not willing to give up or share the political, religious, and economic control that they have enjoyed since the beginning of time.

The next step in the evolution that may have created a significant change in the attitudes and philosophy of sex roles is the development of reliable birth control methods. This, for the first time in human history, allowed the female to act as males do, without paying the biological consequences of pregnancy and the psychological and social consequences of rejection and condemnation when pregnancy came from an illegitimate or undesirable relationship. The combination of birth control and the mechanization of this modern, technological era appear to be responsible for the substantial changes in sex roles. As O'Barr states, "As women are free from an inevitable tie to pregnancy and lactation, and as societal requirements for physical strength are made obsolete by technology, the basis for sexual asymmetry becomes questionable."[88]

Although cross-cultural research has remained limited over the past centuries, the pendulum of international dependency has been moving further toward the development of interdisciplinary and cross-cultural approaches. A number of fundamental questions need to be answered in order to take control of our future:

1. In what kind of world do we wish to live?
2. What direction do we want to take in this new stage of human development?
3. What should be the role of women?
4. What would societies be like if females where in charge?
5. What if the balance of power were not between East and West or conservative and liberal but between males and females?

These empirical questions could be answered by taking a multidimensional approach and by searching for a diagnosis and prognosis of our needs for social changes. An even more important question to be asked is what are our needs for psychological adaptation to the longest revolution, the revolution for equality and justice?

Behavioral scientists should be aware of the underlying psychological and economical levels of development. The first step in the process toward a better understanding of sex roles is to clarify one's beliefs on why sex roles exist and how those roles are being changed by external elements of this highly technological era. The impact of modernization on sex roles is clearly reflected in the world improvement of women's status. "The conclusion which seems warranted here, then, is that while culture has reinforced biological differences in the past for adaptive reasons, the changing nature of ecological requirements in modern life negates the importance of biological differences to survival."[89] Traditional sex roles have to be modified to prepare for the changes technology was producing in the past and continues to produce today. The need for a better understanding of our modern and complex societies requires a multidisciplinary approach. As Peccei reveals, "The real problem of the human species, at this stage of its evolution, is that it has not been able to culturally keep pace with and fully adjust to the changed realities, which themselves have been brought about in this universe."[90]

What appears to be clear is that by working toward greater equality among individuals, we could improve the quality of contemporary civilization on the whole. According to the futurologist, Alvin Tofler, changes in sex roles are inevitable. As he describes it:

> "The typical pre-industrial family not only had a good many children, but numerous other dependents as well—grandparents, uncles, aunts, and cousins. Such "extended" families were well suited for survival in slow-paced agricultural societies. But such families are hard to transport or transplant. They are immobile. According to this phenomenon, the mobile, modern, industrial societies demanded masses of workers ready and able to move off the land in pursuit of jobs and move again whenever necessary."[91]

Now more than ever, traditional cultures are trying to adapt and keep up with the other modern, technological, and quickly-changing societies. Globalization is forcing many people to sink or swim as individuals and as cultures. So far, the most powerful and technologically advanced countries are deciding (in a very authoritarian, paternalistic way) the direction that the rest of the world should take. As in the past, there are some cultures and countries that are passively accepting this authoritarian dictum imposed upon them by the developed countries. However, others refuse to be redefined by the dominant cultures which possess formidable economic and military power. As a result, these paternalistic countries are experiencing rumblings of discontent among the subjugated peoples. The world does not have to be divided into these two camps of master and servant, however. Certainly we would all be much better off if we approached our relationships in a much more egalitarian mode. By reeducating people to simply practice "the Golden Rule," along with democratic principles, we could transform the world into a much more peaceful habitat. The time has come to allow all people of the world to decide the kind of system and society in which they wish to dwell. We need to send a strong message that "Might does not make right." We must start this endeavor by educating people to implement democratic principles and to place more women in positions of power to accomplish this goal.

Chapter 2

Education Versus The "Idiot" Factory

The most important factor in achieving real social and humanitarian change at both national and international levels is education. Ignorance and misinformation are the roots of many of our problems. For centuries, the people in power (usually Caucasian males) have tried to keep the "others" (females and different ethnic or racial groups) from having access to education and knowledge. The reason: power and control. Knowledge is power, after all. Let us now explore what men have done to deny education to those to whom they wish to deny power.

Progressively, during the last few decades, especially since the industrial revolution, a number of factors may have had transcendental effects on gender roles. Scientific developments, such as birth control, mechanization, mobility of society, mass education, and other technological elements, may have produced significant changes in our traditional views of sex roles and human sexuality.[92] But the reality is that in most societies in the world, the obstacles presented to women to be able to make decisions and to act as leaders are still pretty much in place. Those obstacles, in large part, stem from a lack of education for females in many societies.

One of the best examples in history of repression and injustice perpetrated upon females by male leaders was the case of sor Juana Ines de la Cruz, a 17th century Mexican nun who, by using philosophical and moral discourse, challenged the male-dominated hypocritical society. She presented, in a very eloquent and intelligent way, the illogical morality and unfair treatment of women living in a male, chauvinistic culture. In her poem "Hombres Necios Que Acusais," sor Juana Ines de la Cruz said, "Hombres necios que acusais a la mujer sin razon, sin ver que sois la ocacion de lo mismo que culpais" (Foolish men who blame women without reason, without seeing that you are the cause of the sin that you blame them for). She goes on to ask the question, "Quien es mas de culpar por cualquier mal haga, la que peca por la paga o el que paga por pecar?" (And who is more to blame for whatever wrongdoing, the one who sins for pay or the one who pays to sin? In other words, she is referring to prostitution and asking society who is more responsible for the evils of prostitution. Is it women who, many times, must work as prostitutes just to survive, or is it the men who voluntarily exploit and use the dire circumstances of these women to satisfy their sexual urges? Her answer is simple, logical, and fair. Even though both are to blame, men are more to blame because of the hypocrisy of their actions. This is just one example of how the patriarchal societies have managed to silence the voice of reason. The duality between purity and impurity (whoredom) is still one of the most powerful forces used by males to subjugate females. In many cultures there are two types of women: the pure and decent ones (our mothers, sisters, wives, etc.) and the impure and indecent ones—the ones who do not follow the conservative, traditional, male-defined role for females.

Education has become the best weapon to fight against the double standards of society. In countries like Denmark and Sweden, not only do they provide excellent sex education for their children, but they also have managed to honestly recognize the problem of sexism and to do something about it. Today, the Scandinavian countries have the highest percentage of females in governmental leadership positions in the world. On the other hand, even though there has been some improvement in some countries, the majority of countries and cultures in the world are still treating females as second class citizens.

Global education has the potential to be a big part of the solution to the world's problems, as Gail Walker expressed it:

"No effort should be spared to persuade countries to repeal laws and practices that continue to reduce women and girls to second class citizens. Harmful traditional practices, including genital mutilation, discriminatory customs (such as forced marriages), and outright attacks, continue to be factors that make women flee conditions of unbearable hardship."[93]

Knowledge is power. With the understanding of DNA as our genetic identification, for the first time in human history, we can prove or guarantee paternity. Societies that refuse to modernize will find themselves increasingly in conflict with the new paradigms. One of the most important issues in the confrontation between the Islamic fundamentalists and the modern, Western culture is the role of women. Just as for centuries the Judeo-Christian world demanded very submissive behavior for females, Muslim societies still expect an even more restricted and controlled environment for their females.

The fact is that in the traditional, patriarchal societies, the importance of virginity and fidelity has been the ruling factor to determine the role and acceptable behavior of women. The idea of the immaculate Virgin Mary plays a very important role in traditional Christian societies. The Biblical treatment of prostitutes and adulteresses as some of the world's worst sinners is an example of the importance for women to maintain their sexual purity. Other examples that teach women than they must remain "pure" include stoning, chastity belts, and the clerical, conservative clothing of nuns. The Judeo-Christian tradition has had its share of brutal impositions of man's views at the expense of woman's freedom and equality. As expressed by Abigail Adams in a letter to her husband John Adams :

> "I long to hear that you have declared an independency, and, by the way, in the new Code of Laws which I suppose it will be necessary for you to make, I desire you would remember the ladies and be more generous and favorable to them than your ancestors. Do not put such unlimited power into the hands of the husbands. Remember, all Men would be tyrants if they could. If particular care and attention

is not paid to the Ladies, we are determined to foment a rebellion and will not hold ourselves bound by any Laws in which we have no voice or Representation."

In the course of John's reply, he wrote on April 14, 1776:

"As to your extraordinary Code of Laws, I cannot but laugh. We have been told that our Struggle has loosened the bands of Government everywhere. That children and apprentices were disobedient—that schools and Colleges were grown turbulent—that Indians slighted their Guardians and Negroes grew insolent to their Masters. But your letter was the first Intimation that another Tribe more numerous and powerful than all the rest were grown disconnected. This is rather too coarse a Compliment but you are so saucy, I won't blot it out".

Abigail's response on May 7 was as follows:

"I cannot say that I think you very generous to the Ladies, for whilst you are proclaiming peace and good will to Men, Emancipating all Nations, you insist upon retaining an absolute power over Wives. But you must remember that arbitrary power is like most other things which are very hard—very liable to be broken".[94]

As exemplified by the Adams' correspondence, males throughout history have, on some occasions, preached equality. Unfortunately, males have more often than not practiced unjustified inequality.

Thanks to scientific developments, such as reliable birth control, DNA testing, and mechanized, modern technologies, Western societies have been able to move forward through education to achieve a more just, free, and egalitarian society. Even though the "glass ceilings" for women still exist in many areas, a great amount of progress has been achieved. On the other hand, societies that, in many respects, refuse to embrace scientific knowledge and change, still live in the past. From covering the female body and face to the idea of arranged matrimony, some cultures refuse to see (either by ignorance or by choice) that the time of practicing such repressive, inhumane, and unfair rule over females is no longer necessary to ensure paternity. Only through peaceful dialogue, education, and respect, will people be able to genuinely change.

The historical approach of geographical and cultural colonization does not work. The real change, in order to last, has to come from within. To try to impose democracy or any philosophical and political systems on another group of people is usually doomed to failure. History is full of examples in which the dominant group (usually by force) tries to change the way of life for less powerful groups. In the past, there was a possibility to have more than one culture, nation, or empire growing and developing at the same time without having to compete with each other. Today, with the technological advances that we have, especially in the areas of communications and computer science, whatever is happening in one part of the world is instantly known in the rest of the world. Therefore, it is only a matter of time (probably a very short amount of time) before the societies/cultures that live in the past, meet the present and, hopefully, embrace the future.

The argument against change for most of the societies that do not agree with the modern, technological, Western world is the lack of moral authority among the leaders of the most powerful nations on earth. For example, when the U.S. government preaches democracy overseas, but at home only 50 percent of the population actually votes, and the level of corruption and influence of powerful economic entities decides policy, it does not present a good picture of what democracy should be.

The first step toward real progress and positive change begins with the educational systems of most nations. This is especially true in the cultures or societies that are the economic, cultural, and political frontrunners. Even though the U.S. is not the only major power in the world, it certainly has the largest economy, has the most military power, and has a tremendous cultural influence on the rest of the world. It is precisely in this country that is the most powerful nation in human history where the need for a radical change in the educational system needs to be achieved. The lack of knowledge, understanding, and analytical thinking in regards to the U.S. role in the world scenario is one of the biggest handicaps for U.S. students to be a constructive force in the inevitability of globalization. Every U.S. student, starting in elementary school, should have an understanding of the interdependency and differences between nations and cultures. Topics such as history should be presented from at least two opposite points of view. This will allow students to become critical thinkers and to understand and see both sides of every conflict.

When it comes to social studies education, most nations tend to see a one-sided, "good-versus-evil" point of view. This ethnocentrism or "blind nationalism" does not allow individuals to judge history rationally and fairly. The story should not be told as "our heroes against their villains." Rather, it should be told realistically, detailing the good and bad actions of leaders and soldiers on both sides of every conflict. For example, in some countries in Latin America, Simon Bolivar is considered a national hero. He is seen as this hero, fighting for and achieving independence, despite the fact that he committed crimes against humanity by giving orders in which he called for the persecution of any and all Spaniards, regardless if they were supporting the Spanish occupation. This is the so-called "collateral damage" concept which is an insulting term used to excuse murder by leaders throughout history. Winston Churchill ordered the bombing and destruction of the German town of Dresden, knowing full well that the majority of the casualties would be innocent German civilian elderly, women, and children. Only a few decades ago, President Truman ordered the annihilation of Hiroshima and Nagasaki where more than 100,000 innocent Japanese civilians paid the ultimate price of the insane masculine ways of war. Many more of them were condemned to a life of suffering the effects of radiation poisoning. It is important to make clear that by no means are the actions of these leaders to be considered on the same scale as the atrocities committed by monsters like Hitler, Stalin, Milosovich, Pol Pot, and Bagosora.

These mass murderers were not simply reacting to violence with violence; rather, they created unneeded violence to achieve their political goals and megalomaniacal immoral actions.

The historic, violent, and tragic events of human history could and should be exemplified by the Holocaust by having an educational system that emphasizes humanity as "us" instead of labeling Jews, Muslims, Germans, Americans, etc. We could identify ourselves as members of the same family in which we have a small group of corrupt, evil, powerful individuals who manipulate our emotions and actions with concepts or ideologies of nationalism and religion. Through the international organization known as the United Nations, we have taken very small steps toward a peaceful international community, as shown with the authorship of the United Nations Universal Declaration of Human Rights:

> "All human beings are born free and equal in dignity and rights. They are endowed with reason and conscience and should act towards one another in a spirit of brotherhood. Everyone is entitled to all the rights and freedoms set forth in this Declaration, without distinction of any kind, such as race, color, sex, language, religion, political or other opinion, national or social origin, property, birth or other status. Furthermore, no distinction shall be made on the basis of the political, jurisdictional or international status of the country or territory to which a person belongs, whether it be independent, trust, non-self-governing, or under any other limitation of sovereignty. Everyone has the right to life, liberty, and security of person."

We have a long way to go to implement these universal values with which the majority of people would agree. So far, the governments of the world have done very little to implement these values. This is mainly because of the lack of moral leaders and the tremendous influence of the military-industrial complex. Once again, there are theories about brotherhood and peace among people and nations, but there is very little actual practice of these ideals because of the male-dominated, traditional mentality.

If the people of the world look at the present situation, and Iraq is used as an example, it could be argued that there are different factors that contributed to this unjustified and tragic war. The ignorance or lack of historical perspective that the Bush administration presented in deciding what actions to take against the government of Iraq explains the illogical ways that the U.S. government dealt with the Iraqi regime. From the moral point of view, it makes no sense that the U.S. originally supported Saddam Hussein in his quest for power in the 1970's, knowing that he committed crimes against humanity. The U.S. government helped him acquire power at that time and then about 30 years later, toppled his regime. A country is either with or against immorality and criminals and should not be allowed to conveniently select when someone is an enemy or an ally. The people must hold leaders responsible for their lack of moral authority.

Another hard-to-prove factor which must be considered is the psychological, motivating forces that tell a leader to go to war. Most have heard of the "Napoleonic Complex" which describes political leaders who, because they feel inferior in some way, desire to compensate for their lack of power and feelings of emasculation by going to war. This is probably especially true when they have the confidence of having superior weapons and armies. By having a well-educated population, and a democratic system that encourages participation (not along party lines, but rather on an issue by issue basis), it is possible that mistakes such as the Iraq War, which left thousands of innocent American soldiers and thousands of dead Iraqi civilians, could have been avoided.

Most people would probably agree that wars create a cycle of destruction, death, and violence. As expressed by the group, Women United against War, "We make this demand because we understand that warfare creates endless cycles of violence, destruction and death, impoverishing us spiritually and economically." If the youth of the world could, at a young age, concentrate on national and international current events and present as many points of view as possible, then those students could critically analyze the events that directly affect their lives and their futures. It is important to know about the past, but it may be even more important to understand the present in order to build the future.

Going back to the example of Iraq, using a multi-disciplinary approach, the student should analyze the war and its effects on the U.S. economy (learning practical, applied mathematics and economics), U.S. foreign relations (learning geography, history, and political theory), and human rights (comparative political systems, cultural diversity, sociology) in the process. All of this should be integrated into education, combined with the theory and practice of reading and writing skills. This curriculum would be designed to encourage students to analyze, to research, and, more importantly, to try to find solutions or better ways to deal with a given problem. This same concept of approaching different topics using different subject areas would be pertinent and relevant to the students' lives.

Another example would be educating students on the issues of global warming or the energy crisis. If students were analyzing and understanding the sources of energy, its costs, both financially and environmentally, and the benefits and consequences of each type of energy source, then by the time they finished high school, students would know how to calculate the amount of energy consumed by his or her household with its various household items and appliances through the application of basic mathematics. Students should also be educated about the cost of obtaining energy and the source of that energy, as well as what percentage of their families' budgets that energy consumption represents. Students should then be able to acknowledge all of the financial and environmental consequences of the energy consumed in their households. They should also have the ability to compare their energy use to the typical individual's energy consumption in other parts of the world.

One of the most important devices in U.S. culture, the automobile, should be understood by students in terms of the costs that go into building, maintaining, and using a car. A tremendous amount of information and knowledge can be acquired by applying some of the principles of physics, mathematics, economics, chemistry, geography, and environmental studies in relation to the car. For instance, one of the most important points of information about the automobile is that the energy consumed by the automobile is not used primarily for locomotion, but rather the majority of the energy is wasted in various forms of heat, both from the engine and its mechanical parts. Education must be relevant and practical. By the end of high school, a student should be able to:

1. With and without computer assistance, hypothetically balance his/her budget, understand and balance his/her family budget, and have a very good idea of what is involved in the process of balancing the national budget.
2. By using applied math, calculate the percentage of the budget that is used for energy, food, maintenance, water, and any areas where there could be savings, improvements, or reductions.
3. Understand the difference between needs and wants.
4. Understand and interpret statistical data in relationship to his/her life.
5. Have an extensive and practical knowledge of nutrition and the health consequences of his/her lifestyle choices.
6. Understand the different political and economic systems and be able to explain the positive and negative aspects of each one of them.
7. Understand the philosophies of the major world religions, with emphasis on the similarities among them.
8. Comprehensive sex education from a practical, pragmatic, and realistic point of view, based on science and logic. By the time students reach sexual maturity, they should have a clear understanding of human reproduction, venereal diseases, problems and consequences of promiscuity, and birth control.
9. Calculate the amount of energy used yearly by him/her as an individual, the amount of energy used in his/her household, by his/her school, city, state, country, and

the world. Analyze this information and develop ways to reduce waste. List the economic and environmental consequences of not taking action at both a personal and global level.
10. Understand the process, responsibilities, and potential problems of obtaining a personal loan, obtaining a mortgage, and creating the national debt.
11. Every school year, choose and participate in any community service project with clear documentation of goals, results, and analytical evaluation, with emphasis on improvement.
12. Debate pertinent topics that affect the student's life or future. (Education, health care, economy, drugs, crime, standard of living, welfare, poverty, unemployment, international relations, etc.)
13. Learn an international language (Esperanto) to begin the process of becoming a citizen of the world. This idea may take a while to be implemented, but there is always a beginning to everything. It is possible and very likely that in the future, we humans will have a common universal language which will help to promote a better understanding among the people of the earth. With today's technology, linguists could develop a more practical universal language that could be accepted by the international community. Instead of English, Spanish, or Chinese, why not create a modern language that we could call "Humanish," or any other name that is inclusive and not a source of division between humans?

Of course, currently required math and language courses should also be taught, but taught in conjunction with the above equally important criteria. The potential for realistic and major change at a global level is unlimited throughout education. We need to educate the citizens of the world and move away from the traditional, archaic, and ethnocentric educational system present in most schools. We are, in many cases, confusing education with instruction. To educate is much more than to make students learn/memorize facts (sometimes biased facts) and formulas that they most likely will never use. As Neil Postman suggested: "Without a narrative, life has no meaning. Without meaning, learning has no purpose. Without purpose, schools are houses of detention, not attention."[95] To educate, we must analyze the realities and problems that we humans confront and then work together to find and implement solutions. Education is a continuous process which requires the participation of parents, family members, schools, communities, local and national leaders, media, television and film industries, and religious leaders to contribute to and shape the development of young, open, unbiased minds.

One of the biggest problems that new generations have is that at a very early age, they are presented with conflicting and illogical concepts and hypocrisy. We have the parent who tells his children that hitting someone is wrong, but at the same time spanks (hits) those children when they do something unacceptable (but not necessarily wrong) in their eyes. We have the parent or adult who tells children that using drugs and alcohol (which is a drug) is bad, but then the parent uses and often abuses alcohol. We have some religious leaders who preach love and peace but practice discrimination and division. We have political leaders who manipulate, lie, abuse, steal, create wars, and kill people directly or indirectly in the name of patriotism, nationalism, national security, and national interests.

Education with consistency and without double standards is imperative. The only way to stop the endless cycle of violence is by educating new generations about the irrationality and power of the destruction of violent confrontations to solve any political, religious, or philosophical differences. As part of the curriculum in every school at every grade level, there should be a course on conflict resolution, human development, and the importance of peace. With today's technology, it is possible to expose students to personal international relations at a very early age. Classrooms all over the world could be interacting with each other and promoting the learning of other cultures, languages, and points of view. For the first time in history, we can have instant global communication. School curricula should counter-balance the constant information and misinformation about the evils of other countries. Most people agree on the tremendous educational value of our young people participating in educational exchange programs, which certainly contribute to better human interactions and cross-cultural relationships.

Citizenship Participation

From a very early age, every individual member of a community should learn to participate in decision-making and implementation in order to promote the principles of democracy and cooperation. In their curricula, schools should include classes in organization and civil participation in which each student is encouraged to work together with his/her classmates in order to accomplish stated goals. This educational concept could be introduced with simple exercises that allow students to understand the benefits of working together in an organized way and the importance of each individual's participation. An example of this kind of activity could be to have students write their names on a piece of paper and put all the papers in a container. Then have the students, without any direction from the teacher, find their own papers. The only rule is to try to find their papers in the shortest amount of time possible. This activity should be filmed so that later it can be analyzed. After the first part of the exercise is done, students should be asked how they could get the job done in a more efficient or expedient way. One possible way to improve the amount of time and efficiency in accomplishing this task could be to have the students write the alphabet on the board and place their papers under the letter of the alphabet that corresponds to their names. When it is time to find their papers, it would be a much more organized, efficient, and timely process. After finishing the exercise and reviewing the video of both approaches, the students would compare and analyze the advantages of working together in a society where cooperation and organization benefit everyone. By practicing similar exercises, we could encourage participation from all students and avoid the future problem of the lack of participation, due to lack of practice and intimidation by more outspoken and extroverted individuals.

By the time that many students get to middle school, the silent majority simply do not participate in most decisions and student government selection. Instead of democratic elections, we have popularity contests which exclude the average individual. We need to spend maybe 20 to 30 percent of our time from elementary school to high school learning and practicing how to be active citizens so that we do not become apathetic, ignorant, and indifferent adults with regard to our responsibilities and our participation in our democracy. We need to evolve from the nation of idiots (an antiquated, colloquial definition of this word was an individual who did not exercise his right to vote) that we are currently, into a nation of knowledgeable, participating citizens. We, the people, have been allowing the few "popular" politicians to pretend to represent the majority, when in reality the majority of people do not agree with what our current political leaders are doing.

In today's rapidly changing and complex world, participation from a true majority is the only guarantee that the leaders whom we choose are going to do what it takes to create a better future for citizens. We have seen the lack of responsibility, destruction, and instability in the world that most of our leaders have managed to create. It is time to "put our house in order," just as mothers do in most homes throughout the world. Females (mothers) are the ones who usually have clear priorities when it comes to providing nutrition, health, emotional stability, and education for their children. Our home (the planet earth) needs leaders who are seriously willing to listen to and act upon the needs of the majority and not upon egocentric, destructive, archaic, masculine, and greedy principles which are dictated by people with these same characteristics.

Part of the educational curriculum should teach the "value of femininity" if "femininity" implies cooperation, non-aggressiveness, nurturing, love, and peace. Regardless of what we call the package of these qualities, we must emphatically introduce these concepts into the educational process so that the modern, young, male learns to be more (for lack of a better term) "feminine" and, therefore, a better citizen of the world.

Leadership

The future of humanity has never been so uncertain and potentially chaotic as in the 21st century. The number one problem that keeps us from creating a positive and harmonious world community is the lack of leaders with moral authority. The United States, as world leader, has the potential to influence the rest of the international community, if only its leaders were consistent and practiced the basic fundamental principles of freedom and equality, as expressed in the United States Constitution. The double standards practiced by many of our U.S. leaders, especially in relation to foreign policy, has resulted in a lack of credibility among the international community.

Historically, the United States (male leaders), have preached universal human rights and equality for all. Through its actions, however, U.S. government officials (not the people) have often practiced inequality, discrimination, and double standards. For example, Thomas Jefferson talked about freedom for all, but at the same time, he owned slaves. He practiced human ownership, which represents the ultimate lack of liberty. Early U.S. policy toward the Native Americans is another example of amoral behavior. Incidents, like the "Trail of Tears" and the relocation of most Native Americans to less desirable lands, stand out as two primary examples. These moral and philosophical contradictions are the roots for the lack of credibility of the United States government. Numerous cases of the U.S. supporting dictators in many parts of the world do not equate with respecting human rights and the most fundamental Christian beliefs. The leaders of the free world should be the moral leaders of the planet. In order to qualify for such an important position, candidates should meet some basic prerequisites in order to be considered for the job. Among these prerequisites, the potential candidate should be required to pass a comprehensive test which should include:

1. Comprehensive Knowledge of Geography
2. Advanced Statistics
3. Comparative World History (from opposite points of view)
4. Proficiency in a Second Language
5. Comparative Religions (emphasis on similarities)
6. Political Science
7. International Law (theory and practice)
8. Environmental Studies (national and global interrelations)
9. Advanced Economics
10. Diplomacy and Conflict Resolution

To add to this knowledge, the candidate should be required to serve at least two years in the Peace Corps or a similar human-service organization. If a doctor (who is responsible for the lives of hundreds of individuals) has to pass a rigorous test to be accepted into medical school and then study for ten years or more, then a presidential candidate for the United States (who is responsible for the lives of millions of people on the planet) should have to be prepared in every aspect related to that great responsibility. The idea of educating an intellectual and moral individual to assume a position of leadership should also apply to anyone in Congress, as well as all Cabinet members.

Education will offer the path to readiness for future leaders. A curriculum designed to prepare future leaders should be introduced from high school and continuously implemented all the way through graduate school. The selective process for choosing our political leaders should be based on much more than who has the political connections and/or the money to be able to land leadership positions. Many presidents probably would not have passed all sections of the proposed comprehensive test listed above that requires knowledge in areas pertinent to the responsibilities of a president of the United States. One glaring example of a leader who was lacking the knowledge, experience, and credentials required to solve human problems is Mike Brown, the Director of the Federal Emergency Management Agency (FEMA) during the tragic disaster in New Orleans caused by hurricane Katrina in 2005. He was appointed to this position by President George W. Bush and failed miserably in his position during this tragic incident. The sad reality is that because of the lack of proper standards required for leadership positions, politicians practice nepotism at the expense of the people whom they are supposed to serve. Mike Brown in a glaring example of that philosophy which punishes innocent victims because inept leaders and administrators are more concerned about serving their own needs rather than those of the people whom they are sworn to protect and defend.

Finally, a leader should have near impeccable moral character as a prerequisite for his or her position. Besides the integrity of personal moral character, it is imperative that a leader's political record should also be unblemished. To call ourselves civilized, we cannot accept the double standards that paint Stalin and Hitler as criminals, while idolizing Churchill and Truman as heroes. It is true that Stalin and Hitler committed some of the most horrendous crimes against humanity, but Churchill (by bombing Dresden in Germany) and Truman (by dropping atomic bombs on Hiroshima and Nagasaki) also committed crimes against innocent civilians.

The primitive, male rationalization of killing and then using the cover of "collateral damage" to explain away immoral actions is inexcusable and unforgiveable. By no means are the actions of Churchill and Truman as horrendous as those of Hitler and Stalin; however, the actions of any leader killing innocent civilians should be condemned. Let us say that on a scale of 1 to 10 that delineates immoral behavior that the sins of Hitler and Stalin were a 10 (10 defining the most immoral behavior) and the actions of Churchill and Truman were a 3. Then the goal of a female leader would be to achieve 0 immoral behavior on this scale. For it is highly unlikely that most females would engage in or even want to be a party to such civilian massacres.

Chapter 3

Health Care and Overpopulation: How Much Does a Life Cost?

One of the fundamental problems that humanity confronts is the lack or poor quality of health care. Part of the solution to this problem would be to provide the economic resources needed in order to serve the greatest number of people worldwide. For example, in the U.S., the cost of health care is extremely high because a great percentage of the cost goes toward paying unjustifiable salaries, inflated hospital costs, outrageous pharmaceutical prices, and totally unaffordable insurance premiums. Doctors and health care professionals and providers should practice medicine in order to help the sick, not to create a profitable business. It could be argued that there are some doctors who qualify in the description given by Voltaire when he wrote: "Doctors are men who prescribe medicines of which they know little, to cure diseases of which they know less, in human beings of whom they know nothing."[96] The main motivation for some health care professionals has become the ability to make a great amount of money, regardless of the price that their patients and society have to pay.

There is nothing wrong with doctors making a decent salary, but it is immoral that a profession designed to help people in need uses that necessity to charge unreasonable prices. If everyone involved in health care would look at health care as a noble and giving profession, the reduction in prices would allow the system to reach and take care of millions of people who are denied health care services because they don't have the economic means. On the contrary, insurance and pharmaceutical companies deny health care, and sometimes life, to the disenfranchised by charging astronomical premiums and prices in order to obtain exorbitant profits.

In order to solve the problem of a lack of health care for the world's poor and to help alleviate the increasing financial burden for many, medicine and health care should be practiced by professionals who are dedicated to improving the population's health, rather than becoming wealthy. If medical schools in the U.S. admitted more students and decreased tuition, those who have the ability, desire, and call to become doctors could help us achieve that goal. Not only would the supply of healthcare professionals multiply, but the cost of medical care would be drastically reduced. The cost of educating new doctors would be minimal, compared to that cost in a system which views medicine as a "business." A $120,000 annual salary for a 40-hour work week would allow many dedicated individuals to practice the career they love and still have a decent standard of living.

The argument in some countries, such as the US, that the cost of health care is too expensive can be resolved by prioritizing what really matters. One simple way to pay for the "service" and not the "business" of health care is by replacing wasteful and unnecessary "pork barrel projects" that have been called "bridges to nowhere" with hospitals everywhere.

One of the biggest obstacles that we have as individuals and as nations is our ethnocentrism. The idea that our ways, our views, and our culture are the best creates limitations in finding logical and practical solutions for many of our problems. As president Arias of Costa Rica said, instead of blindly following traditional concepts such as socialism, capitalism, and communism, we should go with pragmatism. In the case of health care, the idea of a "pragmatic socialism" could solve most of the problems. The goal of health care for everyone should be a utilitarian one. The goal concerning health care should be to reach and care for as many people as possible. Call this goal socialistic, if you wish, but this practice works and saves lives, at least in the case of health care. Socialism may not be the ideal system for every faction of government or business, but in the case of health care, it is the humane way to provide this essential service.

Why should a price be put on the life of a human being? By eliminating insurance companies and lawsuits, we could eliminate a huge amount of the costs of public or socialized health care. Instead, consequences for negligent doctors could be manifested in the form of medical probation, or suspended health care licensure in the case of extremely negligent doctors. By eliminating insurance and malpractice lawsuits, the middleman is no longer needed. Funding intended for health care professionals would then not be diverted to "ambulance-chasing" attorneys and middlemen insurance companies. One may ask, "What about the victim or the patient who was injured in the malpractice case?" The answer: since everyone is covered by universal health care, the government would pay the bill for treatment of any injury caused by the initial malpractice. Thus, there is still no financial burden to the patient. For any debilitation caused by a negligent doctor, the doctor could be responsible for paying the patient's lost wages and be on supervised probation for a long period of time.

In a few words, the health care industry, from a moral and an economic point of view, should not be a business. It creates a waste of lives, a waste of money, and a waste of resources. If we de-commercialize the practice of medicine and create preventive health care programs through education, then the health care problem is easily solved at a national and even a global level. If health care curricula, including nutrition, diet, exercise, and understanding of anatomy and physiology, were provided throughout school systems, and a nurse practitioner or physician's assistant (someone licensed to prescribe medication) were assigned to each school zone of a certain population, the health problems of educators and students (a huge percentage of the population) could then be dealt with timely and efficiently. That concept would save time and money for parents, teachers, and students. Parents would not have to take time off work to take their children to a doctor. Students would not have to miss class time. Administrators would not have to call in substitute teachers as often, many of whom cannot provide the same quality of education as the teachers themselves.

In the U.S., many politicians are afraid of being categorized as socialists. It is time to get rid of the labels and be pragmatic about finding solutions and the best approaches to each social puzzle that faces our governments. If some politicians were not bought and paid for by the pharmaceutical and insurance industries, these problems probably could have been solved long ago. As a society, we should prioritize, and through our modern, informational technology and education, learn how politicians vote on such important issues as health care. If they vote in the interests of insurance and pharmaceutical companies instead of for people's health care and financial responsibilities, they should be voted out of office and replaced by more honest and responsible leaders.

There is no excuse for the shortage of nurses and other health care professionals in one of the richest countries of the world. With over 3,000 colleges and universities, health care degrees and programs should be much more accessible and affordable to the general population. One way to encourage and get enough people involved in health care programs and education would be to offer scholarships or to implement national and international programs that would cancel an individual's student debt for serving in communities that have a lack of health care professionals. In the famous words of President John F. Kennedy (which are often ignored) "Ask not what your country can do for you; ask what you can do for your country." No one likes taxes, but they can be used to deal with major social problems like health care by taxing irresponsible consumer habits, such as the use of alcohol, cigarettes, and foods proven to promote health problems (foods high in sugar, sodas, and the foods that have gained the reputation as "junk food," in general).

Imagine a trip to McDonald's, for which a salad is presently the more expensive food choice. Instead of having to choose between a $4 salad and a 99-cent hamburger, imagine a $2 salad and a $4 hamburger. Because of the health consequences of malnutrition, the free market concept of supply and demand should be formulated by adding a health factor. The new economic formula for the food industry should be: demand + health = supply. If an individual chooses to be supplied with unhealthy foods, then he or she should be willing to pay for his/her future health care burden on society by being taxed for the cost of that indulgence. This would save that person's fellow citizens from the burden of their injurious overindulgence.

The idea is not socialization for everything but rather a compromise between the two systems of capitalism and socialism that should not be mutually exclusive. In the case of health care, individuals could be individually rewarded in capitalistic fashion for being proactive about their health and saving the general public the costs of footing the bill for chronic health treatments. However, it is a moral imperative that the health care system be prepared to offer help to each and every individual, regardless of socioeconomic status. There is nothing wrong with the concept of capitalism for most business enterprises. In fact, it is a crucial system for efficient progress driven by competition. No one would argue that the harder one works, the more benefits he should reap. Capitalism should be the ultimate system for just about every department and category of government and society, with the exception of when basic human needs, such as health care and education, should be provided for everyone. If someone is interested in money, he should enter a business or finance profession, not health care. The health of human beings should not be used as an instrument for profit. There is too much risk of immorality and corruption by the attraction of easy money. In this new century, people should stop playing the political games of labeling each other a socialist or capitalist, left wing or right wing. A new, pragmatic melting pot of "isms" should be developed for the benefit of humanity.

How can this be done without destroying democracy? This is indeed, a difficult challenge, for the large majority of people are too stubborn to concede any ground to what they view as the "other side."

If people combine their resources, most of the problems facing humanity could be solved. For example, there is an organization called the Educational Concerns for Hunger Organization

(ECHO for short) which is designed to sustainably fight world hunger through education. In doing this, not only are its members fighting world hunger, but they are also promoting good health and are proactively solving the health care problems of many countries around the world. Their philosophy is an old one, and a very pragmatic one: "Give a man a fish, and he eats for a day. Teach a man to fish, and he eats for a lifetime." One of the important and interesting things about this organization is that they do not push any set of ideals or have any hidden agenda, with the exception that it is the basic right of every human being to have access to food. ECHO works in more than 100 countries, providing information and resources to help the hungry feed themselves. Among many of the nutritional plants and seeds that ECHO has been providing and distributing, along with its agricultural information, is a tree called the Moringa tree, also known as the "Miracle tree." This Moringa tree is very rich in a variety of nutrients. It is commonly said that "Moringa leaves contain more Vitamin A than carrots, more calcium than milk, more iron than spinach, more Vitamin C than oranges, and more potassium than bananas, and that the protein quality of the Moringa's leaves rivals that of milk and eggs."[97]

One of ECHO's best-known programs is to send free trial packets of seed to overseas missionaries and development workers. ECHO's seed bank contains over 335 varieties of hard-to-find food plants, multi-purpose trees, fruit trees, and other tropical crops. These plants hold special potential for producing under difficult conditions—where it is too dry, too wet, or too hilly for most crops.

If the concept of ECHO could be greatly multiplied, then the problem of world hunger could be drastically reduced. The potential to solve the world's food shortage problems is enormous, but the resources must be allocated to the right places. Female leaders would probably divert the resources that are currently invested in war toward more practical, humanitarian, and sustainable solutions to fight world hunger.

Another practical solution to malnutrition and world hunger is "Project Peanut Butter." With a revolutionary food formula that includes peanut butter and other nutritive ingredients,

Mark Manary, M.D. (a professor of pediatric medicine at Washington University School of medicine) managed to reverse progressing malnutrition in starving children. His treatment plan has a very high recovery rate (up to 95%) and is extremely cheap. The world has the "know-how," the tools, and the ability to solve all of the world's nutrition problems. What the world does not have is the will to prioritize global resources for production instead of destruction. Unfortunately, the will to divert resources from globally destructive activities (such as war) to globally constructive causes, such as improved health care, education, and the elimination of malnutrition, is missing. We have the tools to make real changes and to solve these social and economic problems. We simply lack enlightened leaders with the will to implement policies that will benefit mankind.

Overpopulation

One of the most important, controversial, and difficult issues that confronts the world is the problem of overpopulation. As of July 2008, world population reached an estimated 6.7 billion people, with an estimated population growth rate of 1.18% annually. At the same time, some of the most precious natural resources are being destroyed or depleted (forests, water, and fossil fuels). Traditionally, the idea of having a large family played a very important role, especially in agricultural societies. The age demographics had to be in pyramid form (a large percent of the population was young compared to a small percent of elderly) so that the young could support the old. Today we live in two different worlds. There those who live in the present (the technological, advanced, modern societies), and those who live in the past (mainly agricultural and undeveloped societies).

These countries that live in the past are still contributing to this rapid population growth with pyramid-shaped age demographics, while the more modern world has been trying to curb population growth and has achieved almost column-shaped or in some cases, inverted-pyramid age demographics. The modern world is trying to impose its views and ideas upon these traditional cultures in third world countries, which often lack the proper tools (education, health care, and birth control) to help them achieve a smaller birth rate. In the past, a couple or family that had ten children assumed that some of them would not survive infancy. This is still true today in many undeveloped countries. Combine this with the need for more labor to work in agriculture-based communities, and there is an explanation and justification for the logic and need for such large families and skyrocketing population growth.

The main resource that third-world countries have is labor which, unfortunately, is directly related to over-population. In first-world countries, retirement plans are based on investments and financial wealth, while in the third world, investments are based on having many children with the hope that they will take care of their elderly parents. This basic, economic, human resource (that has traditionally represented survival) needs to be replaced by a national, global, social security system that could guarantee geriatric care and basic human needs, such as food, shelter, and medical care. By using education as a tool to adapt and participate in the global economy, citizens of the world could benefit from a coordinated effort to eradicate poverty. According to the United Nations World Conference Against Racism, Without taking race into account, the statistics on the status of the world's women show that women have a long way to go before achieving equality with men . . . of 1.3 billion people living in poverty, 70 percent are women. The two most important factors that could achieve real change are education and family planning. With almost seven billion people already inhabiting our planet in the early 21st century and the enormous problems confronting humanity as a result of this large population, how can we afford to deal with a few more billion people (mainly from poor regions of the world) within a few decades?

On the other hand, modern, technological societies have moved away from having such large families to focus on fewer offspring. In most of the developed world, it has become the status quo to limit the number of children in the household to one or two per family. Given the advantages of health care and the reality of urban living conditions, there is no longer a need for large families. Most "first world" or developed nations are already practicing reliable birth control and have managed to slow or stop population growth within their borders. For the planet's sake, it is important that the "third world" or underdeveloped nations realistically begin to practice and implement such family planning practices. The problem, as in many other areas, is that developed nations expect other nations and cultures to accept and/or adapt to their opinions and views without providing them with the proper financial and educational resources and support.

The phenomenon of overpopulation is directly related to the majority of problems confronting humanity. Using logic, it is clear that the more people there are, the more resources are needed, the more pollution and contamination that is produced, the more destruction/consumption of natural resources, the more individuals living below the poverty line, the more crime, the more regional and international conflicts, the more migration, and the more potential for war and violence. As stated earlier in this book, probably the most important solution or way to achieve or solve these problems is through education. If every country in the world used the energy, resources, and money that is currently being used to build and preserve their militaries for educational and healthcare purposes, instead, we could have a realistic impact on these uncontrollable and exponentially growing problems. The people of the world have the means to solve these problems. The people of the world have the "know how" and the technology. The people of the world have the economic and natural resources to achieve all of these goals. All that is needed is the will and moral political leaders to implement these reforms. There is a universal understanding that motherhood equates to a nurturing disposition. Therefore, it seems logical that the ideal group of leaders to begin implementing and putting these reforms into effect is the female gender of the human race.

One of the major problems confronting humanity is the fact that the global population is growing, while the number of available jobs is being reduced by mechanization and technological developments. Responsible and efficient birth control is an imperative if we seriously want to deal with the problems of overpopulation, hunger, poverty, and global unemployment. For several decades, we have had the tools to implement reliable birth control programs on a global scale, but we have failed to give this problem the priority and resources that it needs in order to make a real difference. Education is the answer. We should look at the educational and birth control programs of the Scandinavian countries to realize that it is possible to achieve responsible family planning to deal with the 21st century overpopulation reality.

If we use the definition of "intelligence" as the ability to make connections, we could make the connection that by reducing the obscene amount of money spent on military purposes, part of that money could be used for education and implementation of birth control and reducing or eliminating poverty and unemployment. Free, universal health care could reduce the expenses of the average "first world" families, especially in the U.S. This would allow people to work perhaps six, instead of eight, hours per day. By reducing the number of hours or days that each individual is expected to work for a great percentage of the working force, it would be possible to create millions of jobs and deal with the growing global problem of unemployment. The traditional, "industrial revolution" work day is no longer needed in order to achieve the same amount of productivity. Mechanization and the computer revolution have reduced the amount of time needed to get the job done. Now there is need to revise the old formula that

time=work=money=material things

By combining reliable birth control with universal health care, plus the reduction of the number of work hours (with a decent income), and the creation of more environmentally-friendly, bio-fuel "agro" energy, we could solve most of the unemployment problems of the world. This, in turn, could reduce poverty, which could possibly reduce crime and probably reduce uncontrolled immigration.

Chapter 4

Energy:
The Ecological Imperative

After the tragic accident that has become possibly the greatest man-made ecological disaster in human history (the British Petroleum oil spill), it is time for us to seriously employ all of the alternative energy sources that are at our disposal. The destruction and potential consequences from an ecological, economic, and human point of view are yet to be measured and accounted for. The fact is that we have solutions to the world's energy needs but are simply lacking the leaders with enough willpower to fight for the future of the world's ecosystems that sustain humanity. Unfortunately, monetary profits seem to dictate government energy policy for the foreseeable future. The solution: "Mother knows best." Let responsible female leaders be the keepers of earth.

The bio-fuels agro-energy (agricultural products that supply energy) sector represents a great new opportunity for a new economic product that will help us eliminate poverty. We need to start by defining concepts that should become new concepts in economics. One example is "social profitability." We tend to think in terms of financial profitability, but we also have to consider social and economic benefits. Social benefits are not the same as financial benefits, but they are as important for policy makers and for environmental profitability. Without environmental and social profitability, we cannot have sustainability. So while financial profitability could last for a while, it would be at the expense of environmental, social, and economic profitability. In the long run, that will worsen the world situation and the "mean quality of life" for everyone. We need to understand that social and environmental profitability are as important as financial profitability. A business entity cannot exist on subsidies forever, even financial profits subsidized by environmental degradation. On the other hand, bio-fuels deserve subsidization in the short term. One must understand the difference between subsidizing non-sustainable businesses as opposed to sustainable ones. "Subsidizing" bio-fuels and the agro-energy sector is actually the wrong term to apply to this energy source. This is not subsidization; it is a future investment. Subsidization of a company, a farm, or an economic activity (when such economic activity is not capable of self-sustainability in the present or the near future), on the other hand, is not feasible. Such subsidization must be eliminated because the project will never be sustainable. However, when there is something that requires a "subsidy" in the short term, and we know that this project will eventually be capable of self-sustainability, then the "subsidy" becomes an investment in the future.

The best example of this subsidization of a necessity is the agriculture/energy sector of Brazil. In the 1980's, people were saying that Brazil was "subsidizing" agricultural/energy, which the Brazilian government was doing with the intent of reducing fossil fuel consumption. This "subsidy" of bio-fuel became an investment, in retrospect, because it has now been more than five years that ethanol has been a self-supporting industry and more economically competitive for consumers in Brazil than is gasoline. The Brazilians are the only ones who have been able to speak of success on such a large scale so far. Compounding this success is the fact that Brazil already produces approximately 80 percent of the fossil fuels it consumes. It, therefore, only makes sense that other nations that produce a smaller amount of their own consumed fossil fuels would have even greater success than Brazil. In terms of labor and efficiency, Brazil's energy transition can be looked at in two different ways. On the one hand, the labor required to produce the fossil fuels was thirty times less and, therefore, thirty times more efficient or cheaper in terms of labor than producing bio-fuels. On the other hand, switching to bio-fuel production created thirty times as many jobs as fossil fuel production, which (given the present economy) may be the desired outcome. Of course, given a comparison between wages in Brazil and wages in the United States, bio-fuel production in the U.S. may never economically out-compete gasoline.

Oil is, without a doubt, the largest commodity being commercialized world-wide, and it is being produced by only 20 countries. We must develop a substitute for that fossil fuel, which is contaminating the planet and is the main source responsible for environmental problems that the world is experiencing right now. Once we decide to substitute fossil fuels with bio-fuels, we will create a new sector of the economy to substitute for fossil fuels. This new substitute would and could hypothetically be produced in every country, as opposed to only 20 of them presently. Virtually every country will be capable of producing some source of bio-fuel or some type of bio-fuel, and this system would create world-scale social and environmental profitability.

Furthermore, the fact that the energy that comes from bio-fuels produces twenty to thirty times more labor than fossil fuels creates more social benefits associated with bio-fuels. Hence, this energy solution is also an enormous opportunity to fight poverty, if it is done intelligently with the development of the right programs and policies. Bio-fuel would be a new economic sector which would spring up mostly in rural areas, due to the need for biomass production. It follows, then, that this energy transition would improve the more rural, agricultural communities which are normally the poorer areas of the world. Green energy, therefore, is a two-pronged solution to both rural poverty and the world's energy needs, along with its environmental problems. It only needs proper policies and programs. This is one of our main problems right now in that we do not have any country with the right framework and application for optimizing social, environmental, and economic benefits by creating an agricultural energy sector. As in every other area, women have a lot to offer in this area, since in the agricultural areas, women are already very much involved in productivity.

These are opportunities to convert a challenging crisis situation into a better opportunity for society in general. The bio-fuel industry includes the development of new technologies and emphasis on wise land allocation choices, since harm to the food sector is undesirable. The World Bank is already prioritizing the issue of bio-fuels. They paid a visit to the Dominican Republic to find ways to improve the bio-fuel industry, but there are still no working models that they can use. This is an area that needs to be researched and worked on to produce solutions. Models should be developed that have the wisdom and understanding and that apply a combination of factors and goals that include not only financial goals, but environmental and social goals, as well.

Along with opportunities in the bio-fuel industry, there is also the opportunity to develop new technologies and to use new technologies associated with bio-fuels, such as wind energy or ocean energy. These other alternative energy sources are also usually related to rural areas. With solar and wind energy, one could produce synthetic fuels, which in Italy are equivalent to bio-fuels. The Italians are using something called aqua fuels that are not hydrogen liquid fuels but that work very efficiently. The Indians are already using bio-gas, which is a mixture of diesel and bio-fuel and which reduces the consumption of diesel to one-half or one-third of previous use. We need to combine energy solutions with environmental and socioeconomic programs.

The United States could play a very important role in the development of bio-fuels. So far, countries like Brazil and India have developed technology to solve some energy problems. The main reason for U.S. involvement in the development of bio-fuels in Latin America appears to be political. By developing bio-fuels, many of the Latin American countries' dependency on oil will decrease, and the influence of governments such as Venezuela (which is a government antagonistic to the United States) will diminish. If the approach were to develop bio-fuels in order to help improve the economy and solve some environmental problems, the United States would have the moral authority to be the world's leader.

Another very important source of energy is hydrogen energy. While internal combustion is only 25-30% efficient in converting fuel to usable energy, hydrogen fuel cells are 60-70% efficient, but the fuel cells need hydrogen. Unfortunately, the technology to produce the hydrogen needed for automobiles and to produce electricity is not easily accessible, so for now, the bio-fuels solution appears to be more pragmatic, reasonable, and immediate. We could keep naming other possible sources of energy that would contribute to dealing with the energy needs of many nations, but until we elect responsible leaders with humanistic priorities instead of those who are for sale to the oil companies, we will continue to waste our resources, destroy our fragile ecology, and perpetuate the dangerous geopolitical game for regional and global control.

By diverting some of the military resources (money) to education and innovation in the area of energy, the U.S. not only could minimize its dependency on foreign oil (which would provide more security than obsolete, conventional weapons), but it would also lead by example in the fight against environmental degradation. In addition to the tremendous resources and energy wasted by the military, we could argue that the Sports Utility Vehicle (SUV) mentality of "bigger is better," and the male love affair with the automobile are more examples of how the macho male mentality is contributing to the entropy of our planet.

Chapter 5

Prejudice:
The Price of Ignorance
(Racism and Ethnocentrism)

Many types of prejudice exist on our planet. Throughout this book we have been referring to and explaining one of the most universal ones—sexism. It is also important to understand and deal with the problem of racism as an obstacle to human development.

One of the biggest problems in American society (and many others) is the problem of racism. Historically, there have been too many different conflicts because our society has not been able to deal with this sad reality in a very comprehensive and pragmatic way. In reality, a great amount of racism and intolerance between the different ethnic and racial groups exists in our nation. We are supposed to be the "melting pot" of cultures, but we are actually more of a "salad bar," as some like to refer to it. Different racial and ethnic groups are not really socially integrated but are segregated according to the shades of their skin and, frequently, in conflict with each other because they belong to different ethnic groups.

The U.S. has led the world from an economic, political, and cultural point of view for more than a half-century. Throughout the world, this leadership that the U.S. has managed to promote and use to its advantage is eroding because of incompatibility, lack of moral authority, failure to practice what we preach, and failure to eliminate racism within our own country. Controversy, discussion, and debate constantly revolve around the topic of how much better things are than they used to be, or that racism is a disease that has been eliminated like the plague. Some people pretend that the problem of racism is no longer a widespread one; on the contrary, this problem simply has been put aside and is no longer discussed. People, in general, avoid talking about it and dealing with it, but there is still a great amount of racism in our society.

In order to deal with this major problem, education is the answer that eventually will allow us to eliminate immoral and unfair cultural practices. If children, from a very early age, learn about the actual differences and similarities between humans and between the races, this will help them to appreciate people for who they are, rather than to judge them for small differences that divide what we call "the races." From an educational point of view, the concept of races explained herein should help people understand that the so-called differences among the races are very superficial.

To explain that concept, let's analyze (from an anthropological and anatomical point of view) the basic differences according to most anthropological studies regarding the three racial groups: Caucasoid, whom we call white; Negroid, whom we call black; and Mongoloid, whom we call Asians or Orientals. The physiological differences among these three groups are very small, and the facts presented here will illustrate why these differences exist.

Caucasoids, or white people, are physically characterized as having straight hair, a very narrow nose, very thin lips, and very pale or light-colored skin. The group categorized as Negroids, or black people, have curly, kinky hair, dark skin, a wide nose, and thick lips. Generally these characteristics vary some within each group, but for most individuals these are the predominant characteristics that separate or identify each of these two races. Finally, the Mongoloids are characterized as having very straight, dark hair, slanted eyes, very little facial or body hair, and relatively pale skin. For a long time Mongoloids were also referred to as "the yellow race." There are some combinations of these groups which are referred to in other terms in different languages, but overall, we have now described the three main racial groups and can use these categories to discuss their representations in our American society. For the purposes of this discussion, Native Americans will be included with the Mongoloids. The explanation behind this inclusion is the widely-accepted theory that Native Americans originally arrived in the Americas by crossing the Bering Strait land bridge from their native lands in Asia, prior to written history, and there is little variation within their appearances. Most of their basic physical characteristics are pretty much the same.

To further understand the possible explanation for the differences between the races, we apply a few simple and logical theories. For example, Caucasoids' usually straight hair can be explained by the weather conditions in the temperate zones of the northern hemisphere where they live. In these areas, the winters are long and cold, and the temperatures may fall below zero degrees for months at a time. Physiologically speaking, since straight hair is able to matt together, it can create an insulating blanket to cover the head and prevent heat loss (a great percentage of body heat leaves through the top of the head). Straight hair, therefore, actually functions as protection, i.e. a blanket against the cold weather. In the case of the Negroids' hair, if one observes structure and design of the curly hair, one would notice that in between each curl, there is space for air to circulate, creating an ideal cooling mechanism for individuals indigenous to more tropical areas of the planet. This makes quite a bit of sense, since that is the area of the world in which the Negroid race originated. That particular feature of the hair is a protection against the sun. It keeps the head cool and serves as protection against the extreme heat and burn from the sun's rays. Regarding the nose, Caucasians have a relatively thin nose, again due to cold weather climate. By having a small opening through the nose, air has a more narrow entry passage and, therefore, the area of contact per unit volume for air molecules to be warmed by capillaries within the nose is much greater before entering the inner respiratory system. It follows, then, that having a small, narrow nose is actually a defensive feature against cold weather and cold air entering the body. Contrarily, Negroids (or black people) have wide nasal openings for precisely the opposite reasons of the Caucasoids. By having larger nasal passageways, more air is allowed to enter the nose with less warming capillary contact, which increases the chances that there will be cooler air entering the body. Finally, the lips are one more of the few characteristics that differentiate white and black people and has actually been one of the most significant points of division in the racial conflict between whites and blacks. Once again, looking at the lips, Caucasoids or whites typically have thin, small lips. For anyone who has lived in a northern region, where the weather can get down below zero degrees Fahrenheit, having small, thin lips is protection against the weather. Since lips need to stay moist, physiological aspects and simple physics dictate that the combination of a need for moisture and very low temperatures will create problems. Mucous membranes that are exposed to cold weather for too long can become very damaged. Thus, the lips of white people are thin, as a protection against cold air exposure. On the other hand, Negroids' very thick lips help cool off the body by having a greater surface area that perspires and cools the body through the evaporation of saliva. This feature makes the body more efficient at cooling off in intense, hot weather.

Finally, the most important difference and reason for verbal persecution and racial division is the color of the skin. This difference can be explained, once again, with a little knowledge of biology and climate geography. Caucasoids, throughout thousands of years, have lived in the northern hemisphere's cold climates where the amount of sun is limited, especially during the winter months in some locations, such as Sweden, Norway, and the northern countries where there is almost no sun during the winter. Sometimes those areas experience up to two weeks without any sun. Sunlight is a physiological necessity for the production of vitamin D, which is essential for homeostasis and for the functioning of the human body. Therefore, by having light skin, Caucasoids are able to absorb more sun and, therefore, to metabolize and produce more vitamin D. Under the weather conditions in which most of the Caucasoids have evolved, they developed fairer skin because it was imperative to survive. Meanwhile, for Negroids, who originated mostly in warmer, sunnier climates, the idea is precisely the opposite. Since these hot climate regions have an abundance of sun all the year around, blacks developed the need to avoid sunlight. This was accomplished by producing more melanin (the natural protein pigment of the skin) which protects them from too much sunlight, sunburns, skin cancer, and overproduction of vitamin D, which can be toxic in large amounts. Nowadays in modern society, the demographics of all these regions have become much more heterogeneous, due to worldwide migrations of all of these different racial and ethnic groups. There is now a combination throughout the world of different races living under different weather conditions. We have to see this from a historical perspective and an evolutionary perspective. Under those circumstances, there is an explanation, and a theory behind the differences between these two basic racial groups.

The important point to be made about all of these physical characteristics is the following: given the differences that we've just explained between blacks and whites, the most important factor to be aware of is that those differences represent less than a ten-thousandth of a percent of what a human being is. Therefore, the concept of racism, understood from the perspective of differences between the races, is nothing more than a concept based on ignorance and stupidity. Unfortunately, racism has been one of the worst (and still is one of the worst) tragedies of human history. Through education and understanding, the whole concept of racism could be eradicated, if people learn to see each other as humans who share 99.99% of their physical characteristics. The small fraction of difference could be forgotten, and there would be no more stereotyping, discrimination, and conflict.

There is also an important factor within this entire idea of racism which consists of not only the lack of knowledge, but also the concept of teaching misinformation by pointing out unsubstantiated and illogical differences between the groups to create a cultural division. This cultural difference is, for many people, simply a matter of learning in the absence of critical thinking. If one thinks beyond the whole idea and understands racism as based solely on physical differences between two individuals, it would be an interesting exercise for one to consider: "Could a person who is blind since birth be a racist?" Many people in our society would quickly respond "Yes, a blind person could be racist." These people understand racism as something more than judging someone by the color of his skin, hair type, nose size, or lip size. These people understand racism more as an inherited behavior. When asked the question, "Could you be racist if you were blind," many would answer "yes," which is, of course, not possible. One cannot be racist without sight. People confuse racism with prejudice. There is a big difference between the two. Racism is a type of prejudice, but it is possible to be prejudiced against people for the way they talk, where they are from, or the accents one hears. However, in order to be prejudiced against a race, one would have to see the person whom they are prejudging. A blind person could not be or become a racist. Some might argue: if a blind person can hear a black person talking, then he could identify that person as black and, therefore, could form whatever negative associations with the person that he sees fit. The problem is that this argument is invalid; if this blind individual encountered a black person from England who speaks with a British accent, then he may assume that this person with whom he is speaking is a Caucasian Englishman. No one can recognize a person as being black simply because of his accent.

This discussion presents a moral imperative for the U.S. and American culture. If the people of the U.S. want to lead the world, then the problem of racism must be solved. It is no longer possible for us to pretend that the problem has been solved or that there is no more racism when every day there is a hate crime, or some conflict among the races. Meanwhile, the world community simply watches how the great American experiment still has, as part of their society, the unfair and tragic reality which is racism. Through education, it is possible to finally deal with the problem and change the underlying stereotypes and all the hypocritical double standards our society has. We should ask ourselves, as the first step to dealing with the problem, a very important question which everyone should be able to answer without thinking about it too much. The question is, "Would you be willing to marry someone from another race?" Another question could be "Would you be willing to accept having your children marry someone from another race?" If the answer is an automatic yes, then there is probably not much racism in your thoughts. If, on the other hand, in your heart there is any hesitation, or if you have to think about how to answer, then consider the possibility that there is some element of racism in your mind. This hesitation doesn't make someone a bad person. It doesn't make the problem a permanent one. It simply means that there is a need for more analysis, more discussion, and a better understanding of why we are different, how small those differences are, and how those small differences should not be part of our views of other humans.

In an educational system in which these concepts are included as part of the whole education process, the U.S. can achieve and finally eliminate the evils of racism, which has dominated our society for centuries. The only way that the rest of the world will follow our leadership is if there is consistency between what we preach and what we do, from the Founding Fathers, like Thomas Jefferson, to many other political leaders and creators of this great democracy. It is unfair to pretend that their attitude toward racism and slavery could be justified. There is no justification for someone preaching freedom and equality and at the same time owning slaves. That contradiction is the biggest enemy of our culture and our society because the rest of the world cannot accept our talking about freedom and democracy, while at the same time, many Founding Fathers owned slaves, and still many important modern figures are exposed as racist. It is our duty to teach our children that there is a possibility that we can live in peace and harmony with all other humans without having to include the concept of race as part of our human equation. Education is the solution and the key, and in a very short amount of time, we could take a huge step toward a much more humane society, as long as there is not hypocrisy and intolerance based on physical appearance. By analyzing the sociological, cultural, and political background of racism, it would be easier to understand the need for a much better education that consists of the facts and information we have.

Unfortunately, even some of our linguistic constructs can help to subconsciously embed feelings of prejudice. According to the dictionary, the typical definition of "white" equates white with purity. White is good. White is positive. The color white has a very positive connotation. On the other hand, in the same dictionary, a common definition of the word "black" is often related to negative, absurd, and many times evil, diabolic concepts. It is important to analyze and understand the potential damage that we create with our words, our images, and our figures, which our young people grow up identifying with or looking to as either role models or as objects of revulsion. For example, from the predominantly Christian religious point of view in our society, God and/or the Son of God and other main religious figures are usually portrayed as Caucasian or White. For a child who is learning about religion and God, this concept can clearly have quite an impact. Consider that most children who are exposed to Christianity, regardless of their own race or ethnicity, see the most Supreme Being as White.

Besides the religious and linguistic differences to which Black and White children are exposed, there are also political and historical differences, as far as who has been in charge, as exemplified by the race which has contributed the various national heroes who appear on our currency. Historically, all of these positions of respect have been dominated by the Caucasians. Small children grew up seeing authority figures as being White males. There is no doubt that all of these factors have an influence on the psyche of a child and his developmental process. It is fairly easy to conclude that a small child, who sees the majority of religious and political leaders represented by a race other than his own, may develop the belief that this other race possesses innately superior qualities which allow its members to excel. It is true that things have been changing and are slowly improving, but the basic principles regarding exposure to religious and political figures and the negativity of the word "black" in contrast to the positive attributes of the word "white" are part of every child's everyday life. Only through education and through a fair and clear explanation of the reasons behind these tremendous "achievement" differences between the Caucasoid and Negroid races can fairness and equality be achieved.

It is important to point out that, including this intrinsic concept, there is also the cultural background that is directly related to the historical situations and is directly connected with the language. It is impossible to divorce language from culture within societies. It is also easy to see the difference between some ethnic and racial groups within society. To be fair, it is important to analyze historical background. For instance, we have a stereotype in our society of Blacks and Latinos being loud and lazy and avoiding responsibility regarding paying their fair share and not depending on society. It is very important to see this from a historical perspective when the Caucasians, who were mainly Anglo-Saxons, came to North America. Their main goals and purposes were to have a better life and improve their conditions. They escaped a situation where they were often living in poverty. There was persecution. They were oppressed, so they found a new land, new opportunities, and a potential to grow. The fact that the Puritan religion described work as a way to get closer to God added a religious factor to the desire to work hard. The more one worked, the better off he was. The more people work, the more benefits they reaped and improved their potential to grow and become financially independent. Thus, there was a direct relation between work and a positive future. There was no doubt about the value of work.

On the other hand, when Africans were brought to America, they were brought here under completely different circumstances—as slaves. Many people have declared that we should forget that slavery was ever practiced in America. Many believed that not dealing with it, talking about it, or emphasizing it was the best solution at one point. They felt that it was something that belongs in the past. Unfortunately, the view of the African culture or subculture as and of its people of being lazy have been passed on from generation to generation. Africans were brought to America as slaves, under extreme conditions with all types of physical and spiritual and moral degradations. They were brought against their will. They did not, by any means, want to be here. Now, under the circumstances of a slave, they worked for someone else as many hours as their masters wanted them to work, with no benefits for their labor, other than room and board. In their case, these individuals suffered and were punished for their work, rather than rewarded. This system simply created a mentality of work as a punishment from God. By trying to understand the world through the eyes of a slave (which is almost impossible for those who have not been one), it is easy to see how someone's sociological development and/or concept of the world would be very different than a free person who is working to improve his own situation and to reap the benefits of work. So from the cultural or sub-cultural construct of a slave, the concept of work has been a very negative one for the descendants of Africans in our society. While White people were improving themselves, Black people were suffering from working for somebody else. That is how the main criticism evolved regarding stereotyping against other cultures or races being lazy or not wanting to work. The main thing to take into consideration is that under the same circumstances, any race or group of people would most likely devolve a negative attitude toward work. This perception has been changing slowly, but this sub-cultural background still plays a role in how we see the world.

No one can justify the abysmal treatment of Africans throughout history in our society. There is no excuse in pretending that what happened does not affect what is happening today. The fact that blacks were not permitted, by law, to read for a long period of time in our history is a direct problem as far as their educational experiences are concerned. A level playing field does not exist when we discuss two individuals, one who comes from a family who had the chance to be educated, read, and write, while the other comes from a family who has never been educated. It is not the same for a child who goes home and gets help from his parents or grandparents who have had the opportunity to be educated as it is for the child who goes home and does not have any way to get extra help to improve his intellectual knowledge and capacity. Once again, it is only through education that both groups can solve and really eliminate these stereotypes and differences. There is an expression in Spanish which describes this attitude. The phrase is "el vivo," which means "the one that is alive," or "the wise one," but it also means "someone who managed to get away with something unpleasant," or "something that is not from our desire to do without paying a consequence for not doing what they are supposed to do." This could be a very negative concept in our society today. However, once again, slaves or peasants in most third world countries work for nothing or for a very minimum amount of money. They work hard for ten, twelve, or thirteen hours a day, and they see no benefits from working more or working harder because they do not own anything. They do not benefit from their labor. Under those circumstances, most rational humans would work less or not work at all, if they could do so.

Culturally, the idea is whether one can manage as a slave or as a peasant to get what everyone else gets, which are the basic necessities just to keep living and working. A slave or peasant was smart if he managed to hide or simply avoid working without being caught and punished for it. Most humans would choose to hide or avoid work, instead of suffering and working for someone else. It is also important to understand that the work that we have been talking about is normally intense manual labor, which most people would not do if it were not required of them. It is fairly easy for our society (especially Caucasians) to pretend that this is no longer the case. It is easy to pretend that this is part of history and that we should move on and pretend that we are part of the same playing field. It is important to realize that it takes time for subcultures, concepts, ideas, and people to change.

Another example of the prejudice that exists in American culture is the stereotype of African descendants as being loud. The same stereotype exists for Latin Americans in our society. There is a very simple explanation for the level of noise and how loud a group of people are. Once again, considering geography and weather, the people who came from northern European countries came from regions of the world where the winters are very cold. If people during the winter throughout history spent long periods of time inside cabins, their homes, or indoors in general, then simply by the fact of basic physics, the need for speaking or talking loud does not exist because sound waves bounce off walls and the structure of the building so that people can hear each other with little difficulty. Likewise, the fact that people have to live inside and stay indoors for long periods of time together with many other people could also be annoying. It would be disruptive if people tended to be loud in such confined spaces. On the other hand, the darker people who lived closer to the equator where the weather is warm and people spend most of their year outdoors, actually needed to be louder (based on the laws of physics) to be able to hear each other and to communicate better. Also, the level of noise is much more tolerable, given the space of an open-air setting. Therefore, the difference between the relative quiet and loud natures of these different groups is not an inherited characteristic of race, but rather an environmental, geographical, cultural concept that simply depends on where one grows up and what type of culture an individual has been exposed to. It is possible to argue that one cultural practice is better than the other or that one is right and one is wrong. There is no way to measure what is good or bad as far as how loud someone should or could be. There is a tendency for European culture to see loudness as uncivilized. Once again, this is a matter of definition, interpretation, and opinion. Some claim that there is more happiness, more expression of feelings, and more emotions shared by people who are more out-going or louder about everything, including good and bad feelings. Once again, this is a matter of interpretation, and no scientific or psychological proof exists to support a claim that one is better than the other.

What is important is for people to understand that we are not different because of the color of our skin or our race, but that we are different because of our cultural backgrounds and our environment or specific circumstances. Hence, it comes down to individual differences, not racial differences, and that is the most important factor that should be taught in schools from very early ages. Then maybe we can begin to honestly see each other as humans, without adding the labels of Black, White, Hispanic, or any other name or category that creates divisions and automatic stereotypes, as well as conflicts at many different levels. It is imperative that through education we deal with this problem, that we are honest with ourselves, and that we take the steps necessary to, once and for all, eliminate the curse of racism that exists in our society. By eliminating racism in the United States, which is the leading democracy and the example of what is possible, we may be seen by the rest of the world as the real moral leaders that we should be.

The United States is definitely moving towards a more racially egalitarian society. The best example is the election of the first African-American (actually "mulato," or racially mixed Black and White) president. On the other hand, it is important to point out the fact that much has been made about the race of an individual who should have been referred to all this time as simply an American. Unfortunately, even though some progress has been made toward racial equality by electing an African-American president, real changes will be made only if we elect a president (most likely a female) who will prioritize education and health care by using part of the military budget to achieve social and economic progress, instead of continuing the irrational military intervention in different parts of the world.

Chapter 6

International Relations: The Beautiful American

"Of all the enemies of public liberty, war is perhaps the most to be dreaded because it comprises and develops the germ of every other. War is the parent of armies; from these proceed debts and taxes . . . known instruments for bringing the many under the domination of the few . . . No nation could preserve its freedom in the midst of continual warfare."

—James Madison, Political Observations, 1795

One of the biggest obstacles for achieving peace and worldwide social and economic development is the traditional concept of nationalism. For many years, this concept has been used by stronger nations to divide, conquer, and exploit the weaker or less powerful nations. There is nothing wrong with a feeling of pride and belonging to a specific nation with its own culture and natural wonders. The problem arises when one nation tries to impose its values, views, and interests on other nations. One of the most recent examples is the role that the United States has played throughout the world in the name of national security and national interests. There is a long history of U.S. intervention in many countries, especially in Latin America, where the U.S. has supported dictatorial regimes such as those of Augusto Pinochet in Chile, Jorge Rafael Videla in Argentina, Armas, Fuentes, and Montt in Guatemala, Somoza and his sons in Nicaragua, Trujillo in the Dominican Republic, and Batista in Cuba. There have been many others throughout the world, including the Shah of Iran and Saddam Hussein in Iraq. As he was expressing his disapproval for the U.S. occupation in the Philippines, Mark Twain posed the question, "Can a nation remain true to democratic ideals at home if it subverts them elsewhere?"

Contrary to what many people of the world mistakenly perceive America and Americans to be (arrogant, selfish, and imperialistic, as portrayed in the famous novel, *The Ugly American*, by Eugene Burdick and William Laderer), most Americans are actually generous, fair, honest, and unpretentious, and they have a beautiful sense of equality and freedom. Unfortunately, the image of Americans that people of the world often see is the one that the U.S. government chooses to present, with many legal and moral questionable actions in order to control and dominate other people's lives and governments. The U.S.'s historical support of corrupt and criminal regimes, and sometimes the manipulation of politics in other countries in order to guarantee American influence and interest, has created a negative and often criticized image of the United States of America overseas. We can summarize the lack of moral values of some of the past U.S. leaders when referring to corrupt, despotic leaders of other countries by expressions such as, "He may be a son of a bitch, but he is our son of a bitch." A prime example of this practice is the case of the Dominican Republic's infamous dictatorial president (1930-1961), Rafael L. Trujillo, who was helped by the U.S. government in his efforts to achieve and maintain power by force.

"The famous quote in the preceding paragraph was uttered by *Cordell Hull*, United States *Secretary of State* from 1933-1944. Hull was referring to *Dominican Republic* dictator *Rafael Molino Trujillo*. This quotation is in line with the United States' *foreign policy* during the *Cold War*. Trujillo (as well as many other "*Banana Republic*" dictators) was oppressive, brutal, corrupt and greedy. The people whom these dictators ruled generally lived wretched lives in *abject poverty*, while the dictator, his family, and cronies possessed *wealth beyond reason*. However, as long as U.S. business interests were untouched and *communism* kept at bay, the U.S. placed little pressure on these *tyrants* to *reform*. Often these regimes received economic and *military aid* from the U.S. government."[98]

Many would claim that the mentality of "He may be a son-of-a-bitch, but he is our son-of-a-bitch," is still a major consideration behind U.S. *foreign policy* decisions. People must recognize the fact that what the U.S. government behavior is and has been, is quite separated from what the American people know about what their government was or is doing in other countries. A case in point is the second President Bush's administration's ability to manage, manipulate, and misinform the American people about the role of the Iraqi government in the tragic and cowardly events of September 11, 2001 in New York City and to scare the American people into believing that Saddam Hussein had weapons of mass destruction in order to justify an unnecessary and bloody war. Another example that is not so well known by the American people (ironically also on September 11 of 1973) is the coup d'état that occurred in Chile in order to overthrow the democratically-elected president, Salvador Allende, and replace him with a pro-American dictator, Agusto Pinochet, who, after many years in power and killing thousands of people, was finally brought to justice by the international community.

The following sources verify the extent of U.S. government involvement in what has been the "ugly" side of U.S. foreign relations and the unfortunate misconception that the global community has about the great American people who (for lack of knowledge and their good nature) have been deceived numerous times by their own government.

> "U.S. President *Richard Nixon* ordered the *CIA* to depose President Allende in 1970—immediately after assuming office—with *Project FUBELT*. The U.S. intervention in the internal affairs of Chile was

a foreign policy meant to *worsen* the economic crisis that President Allende faced—in order to propitiate a right-wing *coup d'état*."

United States Senate Report (1975) "Covert Action in Chile, 1963-1973" *U.S. Government Printing Office* Washington. D.C.

"This aforementioned action is further corroborated by a document sent on September 15, 1970 by President Nixon, in which he orders CIA director, *Richard Helms*, to *"Make the economy scream [in Chile] to prevent Allende from coming to power or to unseat him"*

Chile and the United States:
Declassified Documents relating to
the Military Coup, 1970-1976

"CIA, Operating Guidance Cable on Coup Plotting, October 16, 1970: In a secret cable, CIA Deputy Director of Plans, Thomas Karamessines, conveys Kissinger's orders to the CIA station chief in Santiago, Henry Hecksher: 'It is our firm and continuing policy that Allende be overthrown by a coup.' The 'operating guidance' makes it clear that these operations are to be conducted so as to hide the 'American hand,' and that the CIA is to ignore any orders to the contrary from Ambassador Korry, who has not been informed of Track II operations."[99]

If the American people knew that their elected officials were lying and supporting corrupt, criminal, and immoral governments overseas, the great majority of Americans would condemn those leaders and their actions. As a result of this new behavior on the part of American citizens, The United States of America could be, without question, the moral and political leader of the world.

In his article "Terror is Ugly. So is War," Sigurd Hanson describes the tragedy of the war in Afghanistan in which some leaders argue that "Military effort inside Afghanistan should be strengthened, in spite of civilian casualties."[100] In recent reports, the number of civilian casualties in the Iraqi war increased considerably after some Pentagon documents were revealed. It is impossible to know the degree of false information that is given to the American people about the abuses and human rights violations committed by governments in the name of "National Interests." What is clear is that violence and war generate more violence and the lucrative business of war.

The potential for the beauty of the American experiment to achieve its potential to create a more just and harmonious world is in the hands of the future leaders of this great nation. The participation of the American woman is imperative in order to seriously create change. The United States is the most powerful nation in human history. Some people argue that countries like China could become the number one "superpower" in a near future. That premise may be true in a very limited role, mainly in manufacturing, but when it comes to the more important areas of cultural influence, higher education, creativity, economic systems, and the element of multiculturalism, the United States of America has no real rivals. English is the international language for business, aero-space communication, diplomacy, the internet, audio/visual entertainment, and many other academic and cultural areas. The reason that English is the most important and influential language in the world in the 21st century is not because of the British influence, but because of the power and influence of the United States of America for more than a century.

One of the reasons that the U.S. is criticized so much (especially by countries that used to be number one, like England, France, and others) is simply because of envy. The fact that French is no longer the diplomatic language and that the British Empire no longer exists, increases the vitriolic feeling and negative attitude toward the nation that, for better or worse, is the most influential and powerful nation on Earth: the United States of America. As long as we continue to elect incompetent, emotionally-handicapped males to represent us, however, we probably will see little progress to create real positive changes at home and to show the world the real and beautiful character of the American people. The potential for positive change is exponential. By having moral leaders at the national level (preferably a female majority), we not only could solve most of the problems afflicting the citizens of this country, but we could restore the image of the United States as the nation that makes the dreams of freedom, equality, and the opportunity to live in prosperity and peace a reality, not only for U.S. citizens, but for the billions of people of the world who want and need new and honest leadership.

The world has too often seen the "ugly," masculine face of some American leaders who have used fear, lies, and ethnocentrism to conduct foreign relations. Let us now strive to show the world the "beautiful," feminine face of a compassionate, moral, caring and peaceful America.

Leading by example is imperative, and moral consistency is required if the U.S. or any other nation wants to be the true leaders of the world—not by military power but by reason.

> "It is generally true that war is simply incompatible with constitutional democracy. Democracy requires open discussion; war demands secrecy. Democracy thrives upon dissent and disagreements; war represses all opinion not consistent with the aims of the leaders. Democracy is based upon reasonable solutions; war is based upon solutions by force and violence, the greatest possible breakdown of law and order. Democracy places high value upon the individual; war subjects all to a rigid authoritarian hierarchy."[101]

The twentieth century is now defined in large part by the two great wars which devastated many nations and took the lives of tens of millions of people, both military and civilian. This was all done in the name of nationalism. Now that the 21st century has brought all its advances in education and modern technology, conflict should be more easily avoided. As long as we elect moral leaders, we can move away from the path of violence and destruction that has plagued human history. The organizations of the planet should be able to move toward a more universal and peaceful, multicultural, world community.

According to a report of the U.N. Secretary-General in 2008, "The vast majority of 'direct conflict deaths' are attributable to the use of small arms, and as the Security Council is aware, civilian populations (increasingly children) bear the brunt of armed conflict more than ever. Children, especially boys, are being trained to play with or to use either pretend or real weapons as part of their socialization process... The violent male culture translates to the justification of the irrational amount of money spent on the military worldwide."

The following is a table of the top 15 countries with the highest military expenditure for 2009, published in the *Stockholm International Peace Research Institute* (SIPRI) *Yearbook* 2010, using current market exchange rates in current (2009) US dollars.

Rank	Country	Spending ($ b.)	World Share (%)
—	**World Total**	1531	100
1	United States	661	43
2	China	100[a]	6.6[a]
3	France	63.9	4.2
4	United Kingdom	58.3	3.8
5	Russia	53.3[a]	3.5[a]
6	Japan	51.0	3.3
7	Germany	45.6	3.0
8	Saudi Arabia[b]	41.3	2.7
9	India	36.3	2.4
10	Italy	35.8	2.3
11	Brazil	26.1	1.7
12	South Korea	24.1	1.6
13	Canada	19.2	1.3
14	Australia	19.0	1.2
15	Spain	18.3	1.2

[a] SIPRI estimate

As the preeminent economic and military superpower of the world, the United States could lead by example by removing all military personnel from any and every country in the world in which they have a presence. The people of today are no longer living in the times of the Roman Empire, when distance severely limited communication capabilities between one part of the world and another. If the United States chooses to help a specific country or an ally, it could and should be done through diplomacy and/or by an improved system of international law. What is the benefit of the U.S. having military bases and personnel in different parts of the world? Besides the profitable business of anything related to war and military, there is no real value to the current system of international relations. On the other hand, the presence of these military forces in some countries is precisely the argument that the so-called nationalist leaders and hopeful nationalist leaders use to promote their violent agendas of expansion or revolt. These nationalistic and often dictatorial leaders always use nationalism to motivate and mobilize the masses against a chosen enemy. For example, in Cuba, Castro has been using the threat of American imperialism for years to create a veil of fear which he has used to brainwash and control the Cuban people. Using this illusion of a U.S. threat, which the U.S. has assisted in maintaining, Castro has been able to bend the Cuban people to his will.

It is time for a new generation, with a completely new approach, in which peace, respect, and diplomacy are the main elements of foreign policy, to take charge of the most modern and most influential nations. If this happens and these nations lead with their moral authority, they could expect or demand the less developed nations to follow suit and move toward greater levels of democracy and improved human rights. In many cases, political leaders use the international conflicts as a scapegoat to distract public opinion from domestic political and economic problems and to garner further support for their nationalistic agendas and their future political careers. In other cases, religious fanatics and extremists use their religious beliefs to promote Holy wars against the "non-believers" who are, according to them, occupying their homelands. Once again, the simple solution is to remove all military personnel from foreign territory. The economic, political, and moral benefits are much greater than any potential geo-political advantage that had a place in time in the past.

Today, with the technological military advances that the United States and many other first-world countries have, the idea of conventional warfare is quickly becoming obsolete. It has been said that with the creation of the atomic bomb that man has created peace. The basic argument is that until the creation of the atomic bomb, when two countries went to war, there was always a winner and a loser. With the creation of the atomic bomb, it became possible that both sides would lose completely and destroy each other. The world saw this threat of mutually assured destruction fizzle out with the end of the Cold War, but that threat is re-emerging with multiple players on both sides whom the media is portraying as unstable and ready to strike. North Korea has successfully tested weapons, and Iran is nearing nuclear capability, while the world fears that Israel may launch the igniting spark to preempt that capability. These threats come about in addition to the suspicion that non-governmental rogue extremists are at risk of getting ahold of these most-feared weapons of mass destruction.

Now more than ever, due to the potential of nuclear proliferation, it is imperative that the leading nations develop realistic moral solutions. As long as some nations choose to have enough nuclear weapons to destroy the world many times over, those nations do not have the moral authority to expect or demand that other nations not have or develop nuclear weapons themselves. A way to deal with this international problem would be with a serious reformation of the United Nations or with the creation of an international democratic institution which could have the authority and means to enforce international law. If the international community works together and is able to put aside the egocentric nationalistic attitudes that have plagued them for so long and could agree to work toward the benefit of the global community, then global problems, such as armed conflicts, hunger, and environmental degradation, could become the focus of attention, rather than national security. These problems could then all be effectively dealt with.

Through global education from an early age, people could and should be able to differentiate between what the people of a nation desire as opposed to the contrary actions that their government may take at a particular point in that nation's history. For example, the anti-American sentiment in many parts of the world should have been directed toward the particular American government in charge that negatively affected their lives and not towards the American people who, like the majority of the people of the world, want peace and a decent, honest, and prosperous lifestyle. These problems are created by only some governments and their officials, not all of them. Furthermore, all of those problematic governments are time-specific to a particular era in history. The international community should have a way to deal with those governments which, through corruption, violence, and intimidation, violate human rights and create international conflicts in the name of nationalism. Small steps have been taken toward making certain that leaders who have committed crimes against humanity pay for their crimes. An excellent example is the Nuremberg Trials of the German Nazi authoritarian regime, in which justice was served to the worst criminals of human rights violations in the history of the world. A few other leaders worldwide have been brought to justice for their crimes against humanity, but unfortunately, most of these corrupt and murderous leaders manage to get away with their meaningless slaughter of innocent human lives.

One way to enforce international law against corrupt or immoral leaders is by implementing international trade embargos or other economic sanctions, by freezing all of these nations' bank accounts with the stipulation that if they are found guilty of crimes that the money will be returned to their country of origin. Under an international trade embargo, it would be a matter of a very short period of time before a given government would collapse and the country would then have the opportunity to develop. One of the reasons that such immoral leaders do as they please, killing and stealing from the people of their own countries, is that they do so under the shield of national sovereignty. If they were aware of the consequences at an international level, chances are that the corrupt and tragic environment in which the citizens in many nations of the world are forced to live would have to change. It is time to see ourselves as humans of the world first and as citizens of a nation second. It is time to vaccinate ourselves against the dangerous virus that is nationalist sentiment. It is time to leave the past behind and move forward to achieve our full human potential.

For many centuries, the concept of empires and the idea of kingdoms were the predominant way of life or social organization. It is time to modify the concept of nationalism. For modern man, the concept of a kingdom that represents a group of people with a king and queen, a traditional monarchy, is an outdated configuration that has almost completely vanished. Likewise, it is time to change the entire twentieth century idea and international system of nation-states and to move to a new system of an international confederation of world-states so that a few basic world laws can be effectively implemented and enforced. It is important that we move toward educational, legal, and moral globalization. People in some parts of the world still live antiquated lifestyles with ancient and outdated forms of government in which the figure of a king or queen is venerated and idealized. Countries like England still have people who look to their King or Queen as a symbol of pride. In countries, such as Saudi Arabia, the King has almost absolute power. The time of those dictatorial regimes (or the representation of one) should be gone. Global events in the twentieth century proved the need for real democracies based on an educated citizenry who are capable of making informed decisions for their best interests. The time has come in the 21st century for all nations to adopt democratic forms of government which allow for full citizen participation and decision-making.

The global issue that probably has the most urgent need for attention is the state of the inverse relationship between military excess and poverty. It seems ridiculous that the United States and Russia both spend insane amounts of tax money and military manpower to maintain nuclear arsenals that could incinerate everything on the surface of the earth many times over. Meanwhile, sick, starving people are suffering all over the world. Furthermore, an abundance of resources exist to help these people. Vast tracts of unfarmed land are just waiting to be cultivated by the wasted manpower that is now devoted to military operations. There is no reason why agreed upon, complete nuclear disarmament of the world, based upon trust and random inspections, cannot be a reality. Nuclear weapons have become obsolete. The funding for those weapons could be devoted, instead, to development projects by financing an army of workers to fight poverty, disease, and hunger. It would, however, be superfluous for these nuclear countries to create yet another charity organization when there are already too many in existence. It would be best if, instead, the military funds and personnel were given to organizations such as the excellent one known as Educational Concerns for Hunger Organization (ECHO) in Fort Myers, Florida. ECHO offers a practical, long-term solution to world hunger through agricultural innovation and education. More popular organizations, which could have equal benefit and impact, include the United Nations Children's Fund, or UNICEF, and Doctors without Borders.

The recent events concerning Afghanistan have, unfortunately, drawn much-needed attention away from the fight against world hunger and poverty. Instead, the funds and resources that could have improved the lives of many have been diverted toward destruction and retaliation. Terrorism will not end as a result of military operations, arrests, and more deaths, and it will continue to suck resources and efforts into a hopeless attempt at physically dominating people's minds. Terrorism should, instead, be fought primarily through programs that provide food and basic necessities to the people who become victims of the terrorist cult. Relief efforts and other moral gestures of good will can certainly go a long way in persuading people that peaceful efforts, not terrorist activities, will improve their lives. All this is not to say that military operations are completely unnecessary, only that they should take second place in the moral war. Criminals must be brought to justice. The international community must work together to punish all terrorists, not just those who are responsible for the World Trade Center and Pentagon attacks, in order to show that the world disagrees with and will not tolerate the killing of innocents. Only when this is accomplished will we truly have a chance at winning the war on poverty and injustice.

The human race should not tolerate suffering and oppression. These ills must be brought to an end. The world contains enough resources to support every individual, but unfortunately, a majority of those resources are being wasted on supporting vast numbers of troops that either protect their nations against nothing or worsen poverty and living conditions through war. Insane amounts of money have been spent on aircraft carriers, tanks, submarines, jets, destroyers, and small arms, most of which have never been put to use. A much greater, humanitarian cause can be aided with the elimination of this waste. Ending suffering should be the priority. War should be declared on human suffering in all its forms. Diseases must be eliminated, hungry children need to be fed, oppressed women and children must be liberated, and prejudices should be extinguished. Much needs to be done that is not being done. It is time that more of us, as members of the human race, helped each other and took actions to win the war against poverty, disease, hunger, and oppression.

U.S. military expenditures in 2002 totaled $340 billion dollars (globalgame.com). Imagine if that money had been spent on medical research, alternative energy sources, or education and health care, as opposed to producing all sorts of munitions and gas-guzzling military vehicles. One wonders if the U.S. would still be in the economic recession it is in today if its leaders stopped devoting that much taxpayer money to war and destruction. Furthermore, it follows that if the U.S. led by example by not arming itself to the teeth, many other nations around the world would feel less intimidated and may focus, instead, on their many internal problems, such as poverty, health care, malnutrition, and education. According to the Stockholm

International Peace Research Institute Book on Armaments, Disarmament, and International Security for 2008:

- World military expenditure in 2008 is estimated to have reached $1.464 trillion in current (2009) dollars.
- This is a 4% increase since 2007 and a 45% increase since 1999.
- The US is the principal contributor to this world trend, and its military budget makes up slightly less than half of the world total, or 41.5% of total world military spending.

Of course, these numbers are likely far from accurate. In most nations, a large amount of funding is devoted to clandestine operations which are never reported in the national budget. All of this military funding is appropriated for defense, national security, intelligence, and pre-emptive wars. The world spends less than 2% on trying to pre-empt the need for all these costly weapons through mediation, diplomacy, infrastructure development, and decreasing the poverty, malnutrition, and illiteracy rates that are the breeding grounds for these wars. The United Nations is the major organization for such activities.

With that said, who better to represent such an advanced, educated, and civilized democracy than the "fairer sex," as has already been modeled in the Northern European countries that are currently the closest thing to democratic utopias as have ever existed? Women are already biologically, psychologically, and culturally inclined toward solving conflict through communication instead of violence. It makes sense to put the care of the people of the world in the hands of those biologically engineered to care and nurture: females.

Criminal Justice

The double standards present in the criminal justice system nationally and internationally represent one of the biggest challenges to our civilization. The wealthy frequently escape punishment for their crimes or pay less severe consequences for their transgressions than the poor do. The poor individual who commits a crime, sometimes to take care of basic needs, usually pays a serious consequence under the law. On the other hand, the wealthy or well-connected individual who commits a crime can find many ways to avoid punishment, usually by "influencing" powerful decision makers in the legal system.

The large amount of resources used to incarcerate individuals could be better used to implement social programs based on a pragmatic education. Such a plan would create more opportunities for those in lower socio-economic classes and result in their enjoying more meaningful and fulfilling lives. It makes no sense that we spend more money on incarcerating people than on educating them. The first step to resolve this dilemma is to provide an appropriate and excellent education for everyone. After being given educational opportunities, if an individual chooses to commit crimes rather than to earn an honest living, then he must certainly pay consequences. However, those consequences should be directly related to his/her behavior, and appropriate punishments must ensue. Basic capitalist principles should be implemented as a learning tool for the individual, and a fiscal solution to the problem of fairly financing the correctional system should be applied. The basic concept would be to have inmates work (just like everyone else in society) for whatever life-style they choose to live. The quality of food, living comforts, entertainment, etc., would be directly related to the amount and quality of work that they perform. No money from relatives or businesses should be allowed to purchase privileges for the inmates. The idea is that the time spent in prison should include the responsibility to make money to pay bills. The eight-hour work day should be mandatory for prisoners to pay for their basic needs. Any extra hours of work could be used to pay for extra comforts, just as free people do in any capitalist society. Taxpayers should not have to bear the burden of supporting individuals who have committed crimes by their own choice.

By no means should the labor of inmates be used to benefit any profit-earning business or organization. The productivity of the inmates' labor should be used only to support the institution that is housing them or to contribute to society.

For non-violent criminals, the implementation of agricultural and aqua-cultural programs could be educational and nutritional and could alleviate the cost of feeding the inmate population. Another source of income could be derived from having inmates labor in manufacturing industries. Today, because of globalization, there is an intense competition among countries exporting many jobs to countries where labor is very inexpensive. To compete with this more cost-effective, third-world labor, many companies could hire the inmate population and, in return, get some tax relief. They would not exploit the labor of the inmates but would be providing a way for the inmates to learn, to take responsibility for their crimes, and to repay society for their mistakes.

The fact that more than 90% of violent crimes are committed by males gives us an indication of the potential for social development, if we were to use educational programs to teach our boys not to be aggressive but, instead, to avoid violence. From the psychological point of view, it could be argued that most males are "emotionally handicapped." The idea that humans cry as babies and young children, but that after a certain age boys are not supposed to cry, is a contributing factor to the development of this artificial concept of masculinity. By not allowing his feelings to be expressed and pretending that he is fine, the traditional male accumulates negative feelings like anger and frustration. Nature designed humans with the ability to cry in order to release stress and negative feelings. Males are culturally deprived of doing so, resulting in many negative psychological consequences as a result of that cultural practice. Imagine the level of toxicity that would accumulate in our systems if we were to avoid going to the bathroom as frequently as needed. This analogy may not be the best one to make this point, but who is to say that the "emotional toxicity" created by physiological and psychological restraint is not seriously affecting our ability to solve some of our conflicts. The next time that you are watching an emotional movie, look at the males around you and observe the physical struggle to avoid crying. Violence is multiplied when an individual does not or cannot deal with internal or external conflicts by using reason. Historically, we could argue that the show of emotions, especially by males, could have been counter—productive in dealing with threats from other individuals or groups. The appearance of emotional strength was a psychological advantage. Today, with institutions that provide law and order, the need for self defense is less important for survival. The perpetuation of a violent culture by movies, television, and violent sports, only adds to unreasonable, conflictive, and destructive behavior.

At the international level, we know that in many cases, heads of state and high level government officials commit horrendous crimes against humanity and manage to go unpunished for these actions. From human rights abuses to genocide, political and military leaders do as they please, hiding under the excuse of "national security" or the shield of national sovereignty.

It is imperative that the international community seriously demand and implement international laws that have to be obeyed by everyone. The problems of inconsistency and lack of enforcement should not keep the world's leaders (who have the moral authority) from achieving this goal. The number of dictators and so-called democratic leaders who abuse human rights and disregard international law is part of the problem that stands in the way of achieving progress and justice. Teaching by example is the way to make real change. How can we expect the average individual to follow the law and respect human rights if our leaders not only violate human rights guidelines but regularly get away with their horrendous actions, as well?

On the other hand, females, who are taught to release their emotions, exhibit much less violent behavior than males. They are rarely incarcerated, and most spend their lives as productive citizens who raise families. It stands to reason that if we want to recruit moral, productive leaders for the world, we should look among the ranks of women.

Chapter 7

Values, Religion, and Culture

In order to achieve our goals as individuals and as nations, we should define and prioritize our values. Many political and religious leaders not only do not practice what they preach, but they also morally contradict the ideas they are supposedly representing. We humans tend to rationalize our actions and behaviors in order to call ourselves citizens or Christians or Americans without an honest and clear understanding of the meaning of those words. As someone once said, "Going to church on Sundays doesn't make you any more of a Christian than sitting in a garage makes you a car." We must teach, by example, that if someone chooses to be a Christian, then he should practice the Christian philosophy of love and peace every day and all the time. The rule applies to most other major religions which preach peace and brotherhood but do not always practice what they preach. Many religious leaders preach peace and harmony one minute and are supporting physical wars against other ideologies the next. When it comes to morality and values, an individual either believes in the idea that killing is wrong or believes that killing is acceptable. The rationalization of killing in the name of ideologies or nationalism is an excuse to be dishonest with themselves and dishonest with their followers. As Gandhi once said, "There are many causes that I am prepared to die for, but there are no causes that I am prepared to kill for."

In our modern, technological world, the amount of conflictive information that our children are bombarded with makes it even more imperative that children see our national and religious leaders practicing what they preach. When aggressive, violent, destructive video games and popular sports such as Ultimate Fighting, as well as most movies and television, promote or glorify the opposite values that our democratic leaders are supposed to represent, it is no wonder that the nations of the world are being led every day into more and more armed conflicts. Once again, we must attempt to answer one of the most important questions about the human psyche, "Are we a product of nature or nurture?" If we believe that nature plays the most important role in determining human behavior, then we could explain that, due to the hormonal differences between males and females, males tend to be more aggressive, violent, and biologically designed for bellicose behavior. If, on the other hand, we believe that nurture or learning is the main influence on human behavior and education is valued as it should be valued, then we should not allow our children to be influenced by, exposed to, or learn from these destructive and violent games, movies, and sports. Our values and behaviors are shaped by our culture, our language, and our environment. If, as a society, we emphasize values that promote peace, cooperation, and harmony, we should rethink or redesign the negative influence that these traditionally, predominantly-male sports and activities have on our children's development.

Like any culture, the American culture has many positive, constructive, and humanistic aspects, but there are also some areas that are in many ways negative and are the cause of many social problems. Although much progress has been made, the people of the United States are still dealing with the negative impacts of racism, sexism, and exaggerated ethnocentrism and materialism. We have attempted to explain the reasons and possible solutions for most of these problems, with the exception of the latter. When it comes to materialism, we have become more and more attached to and dependent upon material things for happiness. We have become a society in which almost everything that matters is disposable, and money and material things have become almost godlike in many people's minds. We believe that through education we should analyze and understand our values, and concentrate on the importance and value of human relations. We are so busy working to produce money to buy material things that we have neglected the most precious human asset, which should be time with others and for others.

One of the worst rationalizations for not spending more time with one's own children, which is frequently used by many parents in our modern, technological society, is that the quality of a relationship is more important than the quantity of time spent with someone. Hence, the term "quality time" has become a popular expression and excuse for not spending much time with family. We strongly disagree with that idea. We believe that both quality and quantity are extremely important for the welfare of family, neighbors, and overall human relations. We have become slaves of time, where time equates to money and material things. In our modern, materialistic societies, we are so busy making money (to buy material things) that we have very little time for human relations. It has been said that "Money does not buy happiness." In many cases, money is the cause of unhappiness for many people in the world. Money, intelligently and morally used, could also be the source of solutions. A simple formula can illustrate this concept:

> Work + time + money = material objects. At the same time, "time" = quality in human relations.

Only through education and re-evaluation of our moral and human priorities can we change this erosion in the quality of human relations. By teaching the importance of community service at a very early age, and by teaching the importance of altruism, we could reshape the conflictive and negative direction that our modern society has taken. By prioritizing what we really need and not what we want, we could have more time for our children, friends, neighbors, and, in many cases, for our forgotten parents. It is a sad reality when we believe that progress is represented by "warehousing" our elderly in institutions. They may have all of the material things that they need, but in many cases, they lack the most important elements of life, which are love and human relations. Convenient nursing homes or "old folk's homes" can be compared to elephant cemeteries where the sick and the old go to die *en masse*. We modern societies should revise and relearn some of the old values from the so-called less advanced societies which take care of their elderly, rather than storing them away and forgetting about them. From a biological standpoint, humans are designed so that for the first few years of life, they are 100% dependent upon parents for survival. In this wise design, by the time parents grow old, children should have matured to the point that they are then able to take care of their dependent parents. This beautiful, biological, physiological, and psychological arrangement in nature has been broken in the name of a false sense of independence and self-reliance.

If we put more value on time as a way to improve our human relations, it is possible that we can solve one of the biggest problems world-wide, which is unemployment. The traditional concept of an eight-hour work day is an arbitrary idea that doesn't necessarily make sense. By changing the eight-hour work day to a six-hour work day or the five-day work week to a four-day work week, people would have more time for their families, friends, or community service. By reducing the amount of time spent at work for each employee, more jobs could be created for more people. It is a simple formula. The less time per person for work, the more work available for everyone, and the more time available for all people to enjoy with other people. If people value their time with their families more than they value the fourth television in their households, not only would it improve their relations and quality of life, but it would allow millions of people to have the opportunity to make a living.

We must be selective about what works and what is good for humanity and reject what is destructive and negative from our past and from our modern, advanced society. It is time to design a new culture by combining what works to improve the conditions and standards of living for all humanity. So let us stop labeling ideas as socialist, capitalist, communist, developed, or underdeveloped, American, Chinese, or Middle-Eastern.

Let us stop labeling entities by political or cultural identities. Let us break down borders and start referring to entities by the pragmatic and positive qualities that they represent. Who better to lead us into such a pragmatic new age than female leaders with their maternal instincts and indestructible motivation to keep their families together in a caring environment? Who better to change society's largely-male, aggressive attitude into an attitude more geared toward communication and understanding than the mothers of our world?

Religion and Culture

No one religion should forcibly impose its views on society. Instead, each religion should merely emphasize the common beliefs of love and peace. We need to have some conventional and universal moral standards that include all religions' points of view. A minimum moral code that we can all accept (universal commandments) should be developed by representatives or moral leaders from all different religions. The idea of some basic principles, such as freedom of religion, tolerance, commitment to non-violence, mutual respect, etc., must be included in this moral code. Religions, instead of being part of the problem (as they are presently), could be part of the solution to the world's woes. Those who proselytize and try to convert others to a particular religion (insisting that their religion is the one and only real one) have created more conflicts and divisions than they have united people together in peace and love.

In his book, The End of Education, Neil Postman explains that the importance of education is to allow the students to understand, compare, and respect different points of view. As he stated: "I knew that Jews believed their God had parted the Red Sea, and Christians believed their Savior died and came back to life. I was puzzled about why our teacher called the story of Greek gods 'myth' but, I felt sure, would not so designate our own stories."[102]

When reading the basic teachings of the major religions, we can see how the sacred books of Christians, Jews, Muslims, Buddhists, Hindus, and others, have all taught fundamental human rights and peace. By using education as a universal tool, and by teaching the similarities and peaceful messages of all of these religions, the potential for understanding, tolerance, and peaceful co-existence will result and be the base for a more humane society. Let us expose and promote the ethical values that all religions share, instead of concentrating on the differences or preaching about which one religion is the true or best one. We should promote cooperation, and not confrontation, between different religious views. The final decision regarding which specific religion or denomination is correct should be based on an individual's choice, after developing knowledge and understanding of the different points of view.

If we view history from a religious point of view, we can find that practically all of the religions have had their fair share of fanaticism and horrible acts of abuse, cruelty, and injustice toward "non-believers." From the Spanish Inquisition to the acts of terrorism that can be best exemplified by the killing of innocent civilians on September 11, 2001 in the World Trade Center in New York City, the excuse of criminal actions in the name of "holy" goals is nothing but an immoral and tragic distortion of religions that practice the opposite of those religions' true message. The concept of killing in the name of God is incompatible with the basic moral principles of the religions in conflict. We need to teach and explain the errors and "sins" of each one of these religions in order to take historical responsibility for everyone's violent and destructive behaviors. Only then can we begin to seriously work toward an interrelationship based on tolerance and harmony.

President Carter described universal desire for peace when he stated: "The tragedy at Sabra and Shatila, and the events leading up to it, vividly demonstrated the complex interrelationship that have long frustrated those who seek peace in the region . . . The final toll was more than 1400 dead and missing, most of them children, women, and the aged." He went on to describe: "A shocked world responded with condemnation and revulsion . . . Nowhere, however, was the reaction more angry or anguished than in Israel's democratic society."[103] The people of Israel, just like the people of Palestine, want and deserve peace. As long as traditional male religious and political leaders have the power to decide, the chances for peace are very limited. If, instead, the Jewish and Palestinian women were in charge, the probability of serious negotiation and long-lasting peace could be achieved.

As part of the phenomenon of globalization, with its goods and evils, we should include the teaching of a new world view of religion, not for one religion to prevail over others, but to make every religion respected and identified by common goals and common values. This would teach more tolerance and would separate religious belief from political and economic interests. After all, there is usually confusion and misunderstanding between what political, economic, and religious leaders want and what most of the major religions, such as Christianity, Judaism, and Islam, actually preach.

Traditional religions do not deal with many issues that are part of our modern world. We struggle every day with major questions regarding modern technology. Where can technology take us? What are and should be the limits and possibilities of technology? What are the responsibilities? What should we do with technological creations? Those questions were never addressed by the world's major religions because such technology did not exist at the time that the great prophets were disseminating the messages of the great religions. We now have to ask ourselves, "Is technology part of the equation of the human future?" With new developments in areas such as genetic engineering, we do not know how to morally deal with new discoveries and inventions. We have to be humble and realize that some aspects of religion may be obsolete when we are dealing with our modern, technological world.

The conflicts between the rigid traditional ideologies and the modern world are part of the chaotic geo-political world that we live in. In his book "Our Endangered Values", President Carter describes the problem with some fundamentalist leaders: "Almost invariably, fundamentalist movements are led by authoritarian males who consider themselves to be superior to others and, within religious groups, have and overwhelming commitment to subjugate women and to dominate their fellow believers."[104]

The main issue for religions should be to find the common wisdom to respect and practice tolerance among ourselves. Let us globalize and set common values within religions without trying to impose our religious views on each other. Through education, let us discredit the violent and conflictive ideologies of extremist, fundamentalist adherents from all religions and teach the basic common religious philosophy of love and peace. From conflicts between Catholics and Protestants in Ireland, to Hindus and Muslims in India, to the most tragic conflicts between Jews and Muslims in the Middle East, male aggressive behavior must be replaced by a nurturing, peaceful, feminine approach. The historical, irrational conflicts based on religion, dominance, and forceful practices no longer belong in our civilized societies.

Religious messages have tremendous power to heal or to hurt and to create conflict or peace. Unfortunately, throughout history, religion has been and is still used, on too many occasions, as a way to subjugate females and exert political and psychological control over individuals and nations. It has been and is still used as a brain-washing tool to promote violence and terrorism in order to achieve power. Historically, religious leaders have been males who have chosen the use of force to impose their views and rules upon others. It is time for females to be part of the religious leadership who practice what they preach (love and peace), without the hypocritical rationalization to justify discrimination, oppression, and war in the name of God.

Chapter 8

Globalization and Nationalism

If the world ever hopes to achieve any modicum of peaceful survival and tolerance, then we must globalize education, values, and standards for our judicial systems. At present, we are, instead, globalizing commercialism and letting Hollywood, USA globalize our cultures. Anyone who indulges in the frequent viewing of Hollywood's film products realizes that this industry should not be creating global culture. Instead, we need to design a global educational system that can counteract the negative, materialistic, violent culture presented by the film and television industries. When we popularize films which depict the killing of police as acceptable, or popularize the obscene, deplorable, and irresponsible behavior presented on television shows, such as *Jerry Springer*, as part of our culture, we are moving backwards toward a less tolerant and less civilized society. No wonder some other cultures tend to reject (sometimes by aggressive means) the influence that our modern, Western culture has to offer. Consider for a moment how, a century ago, our society would have reacted to the level of violence, degradation, and immoral behavior presented to our children by the modern media. As a society, we must take control of our destiny by using education to promote universal values based on human dignity and peace.

In order to achieve real interdependence and fair globalization, the developed nations need to share the knowledge and opportunities for a more balanced economic, intellectual, and social global community. For decades, the "brain drain" has greatly contributed to the widening economic gap between first and third world nations. The best example of the problem that developing nations have in achieving a level of competitiveness is in the area of intellectual property rights, which we will attempt to explain and connect to the need for real, honest leadership and the possibility of progress. The phenomenon of globalization has been progressing with inequalities that are so vast that it is unrealistic to say that globalization is creating a fairer world. The gap between the developed and developing nations does not allow for fair and healthy competition. This obstacle is very evident in the area of intellectual property rights, where most of the developed nations have a monopoly on modern technology. As presented by Doroteo Rodriguez:[105] The reality is that in the information age that is shaping the 21st Century, Intellectual Property Rights (IPR's), in actual or potential new forms, could become the real economic, working capital (sort of a new world currency) of the future. They could, perhaps, have much more potential for better and fairer socio-economic development than all previous efforts in the evolution of 'capitalism' and 'Western' (modern) civilization.

We live in the Post-Cold-War World. This is a world in which the socialist idealism of "planned economies" collapsed—mainly because of their disregard for the economic validity of private property and private initiative (entrepreneurship) as basic forces of economic development. In this Post-Cold-War world, the collapse of the socialist system has been understood as the success of the "free-market" system, and therefore, it has fostered a strong and universal rhetoric of the benefits of "free competition" and "free global trade," without regulation. The speech in favor of all-beneficial (and inevitable) globalization is becoming common language for politicians and policy makers, to the point that goods and merchandise will deserve and receive more freedoms and rights than many of the citizens who manufacture them.

The World Trade Organization (WTO) appears, then, as a world-enforcing police system, to which all countries (especially undeveloped or developing ones) must comply or submit to, or be ready to be sanctioned and excluded from world trade and international financing and sources of hard currencies. Or they may be excluded from international aide policies, "vital foreign-investment sources," initiatives, and so on. Uncooperative developing nations are quickly excommunicated from resources and technologies vital to a modern nation's survival. The rhetoric about the need for dismantling all market barriers is presented above all considerations.

The immediate or inevitable benefit for the consumer is presented as the supreme priority. Consumer needs (minimum price and maximum quality of goods) become prioritized over any other economic entity (the creator, the entrepreneur, the worker, the farmer, the teacher, the environmentalist, the unemployed, the retired, etc.) without much thought to the essential fact that they are all the same entity. The consumer and economic policies should harmonize every entity's interests and pursuits, since one cannot have the first entity (consumers) in the absence of the others. After all, an individual needs income to be a consumer. China is a prime example of the pragmatic approach to a win/win solution to lift people out of poverty.

One would like to see an equivalent effort (as that which is placed on this free-trade enforcement) to enforce real antitrust laws in the midst of the gigantic mergers that take place all over the world among multinational corporations as thousands (sometimes hundreds of thousands) of employees lose their jobs in a moment. Also, we can observe a local and international increase of oligopolistic structures of economic expansion taking place in the private sector at every economic level, with no real complaints or policies being "enforced" to reverse this process, from the international organizations that procured the enforcement of IPRs so diligently in the last decade. Why this asymmetry? The World Trade Organization (WTO) rounds of negotiations and conferences (Uruguay, Marrakech, Seattle, Prague, etc.) have been the initiatives and persistent pursuits of supposedly the more developed countries. However, some authors and analysts (rarely heard) are warning us that the real driving force behind this process of "global-free-trade" enforcement and rhetoric are the interests and influential power of the multinationals.

This rhetoric of "free-trade-above-all" has become the sort of new, blind ideology substituting the confrontational ideologies and dogmas (left vs. right) of the Cold War era. Needless to say, in all of these free-trade negotiating rounds and efforts, the second (ex-socialists bloc) and third-world states are not well-prepared to negotiate, for evident reasons. The developed world has the dominant position in most important aspects and in many apparently unrelated ones, too. To put it mildly, it has the real negotiating "experts" (the abuse of "dominant position" in terms of economic jargon).

At first glance, we can see that the agenda of globalization is not one of real concern for proper and fair world development and the people's welfare. It is not an agenda for which the minimum global goals in education, health, universal environmental and labor policies, judicial policies and systems, human rights, etc., will be procured and demanded as a priority, alongside the economic aspect. Likewise, neither will such minimums be set forth in terms of standards with respect to access to universal factors of production, like the cost of financing capital, energy, technologies, etc., in order to provide a minimum of conditions under which to compete in fair competition in global economic markets. Nevertheless, an all-out competition has already begun among all countries. Globalization sequence should have started aiming at globalizing cultural, ecological, and social-justice values first, along with a minimum of standards and similar access to factors of production second, and market interests and free global competition third, not the other way around, as seems to be more the case.

However, the above-mentioned sequence has not been the case, likely because these globalization policies did not really spring from "the peoples of the world" or their communities and forums, but rather from the strategic headquarters of the multinational corporations. Although this may sound like a conspiracy theory, one should not regard this phenomenon lightly, since it is easy to lose real perspective; rather, let us keep in mind that any one of the ten largest corporations in today's world have a larger annual value of gross income than probably the whole external sector (imports and exports) of the gross national product (GNP) of each one of the poorest 50 countries in the world combined. Do we see the real picture? Surely, the top ten chief executive officers (CEO's) of these few corporations can agree to achieve a common agenda for the 50 or 100 poorest governments, not to mention the aggregated people of such dissimilar countries, if such were the case to be pursued.

Globalized competition is then pretended and procured in the midst of abysmal differences between countries and "worlds" and, of more concern to our inquiry, in the middle of a perpetual technological innovation process that has transformed industry, economies, and the conditions of production at an unhinging velocity. In ancient times, a successful and generalized invention or innovation had a valid, useful life of centuries, market-wise; since the industrial revolution, however, innovative technologies have reduced their useful life to only decades, at most. Presently, with the electronic and information revolutions, the valid life-span of most technologies is becoming obsolete in just a "lustrum" (half decade) or even months.

This simple but undeniable reality should have had vital implications in the most recent World Trade Organization negotiations rounds and is even more relevant in the realm of intellectual property rights related mainly to technology. Nevertheless, we do not see any signals that such aspects and their implications are being considered on proper grounds—not on the side of the enforcers, the complying (or complaining, if you prefer to call them) countries, or even the patent system. This is certainly one of the main aspects motivating this inquiry about addressing and foreseeing needed changes and the potential of IPR's as a system, as an institutional technology that has to re-invent itself on the grounds of becoming (like all other technologies now more than two centuries old) obsolete, if it does not do so.

The reluctance, resistance, and complaints of most third world countries (and even second world ones, such as the previously Sino-Socialist bloc) with respect to the urged agenda of international organizations towards globalization is perceived or portrayed as another step of "economic imperialism," in the view of many people in developing countries. Needless to say, even within developed countries, one finds similar cries and accusations, although "imperialistic" accusations and arguments are very much discredited as pure, outdated resentment of leftist traces. However, those of us who were never leftists in the Cold War era, should, therefore, dare to speak now about imperialism, not necessarily as evil, but as a real-life factor of historical presence, conspicuously ubiquitous all throughout history, and ubiquitous in a real global sense today, but more than ever associated with technology. It is, therefore, our concern—and our duty—to speak out about it.

Examining history, one discovers that each and every empire was made possible by relying or leaning upon the knowledge and dominion of a superior technology on the side of the dominators, much more than leaning/relying upon character, population, or territorial superiority. Dominion of some populations over others was made possible by a superior knowledge and dominion of material technology (agriculture, metallurgy, mining, carpentry, architecture, etc., that is, the material transformation capacity), now referred to as HARD TECHNOLOGY or by the superior knowledge and effective dominion of the organizational technologies (politics, military, judicial, educational, commercial, etc.), now called SOFT TECHNOLGY in some circles. Usually, the great empires were based on a superior knowledge and dominion of an optimal combination of both technologies.

Each empire, be it Mongol or Persian, Greek or Inca, also had a gravitational center attached to a political identity, a cultural-territorial nationality that identified and sustained it.

The Roman Empire relatively did not "invent" material technologies but learned, combined, and improved upon that of almost all of the people whom it conquered. The base of its immense success and dominion was much more in its capacity to create and dominate organizational technology (soft-technology in today's parlance). For instance, Roman postal roads and communications systems were incomparable. More importantly, however, its military organization and effectiveness and its legal system was stellar. In most "Latin" countries, Roman law is still used as the basis (precedents) for the study of law and jurisdiction. As a matter of fact, British Common Law and United States Law use Roman Law as the underlying structure of their legal systems. Along those same lines, the British Empire was the first to develop and implement the soft technology which has been very successful in stimulating or promoting the creation of hard technology. They also developed the patent system to protect that new technology. Soft technology was then quickly copied and implemented—without any external enforcement—for those other countries more willing to compete in the dominant markets of the time.

Soft technology, also known as institutional technology, has been furiously implemented ever since that time. It has always been a capitalist tool, used to advance wealth and improve lifestyles. As a matter of fact, we are now inundated with an avalanche of technological innovations that do not even give us time to become accustomed to them before the next wave of inventions hit the market place, rendering our most recent innovations obsolete before we can even learn how to properly use them. The legal patent system, however, allows only those who have patent right to materially benefit from their inventions in exchange for divulging and disseminating these marvelous innovations. As a result, a very inequitable living pattern is created, with technologically advanced countries enjoying an unprecedented standard of living, while people who have no patented inventions live much as they did 100 years or more ago.

No doubt this was one of the key historic causes driving the "industrial revolution" that followed the implementation of the patent system and the successive layers of technological revolutions that have followed since: internal combustion, electricity, aviation, telecommunications, electronics, biotechnology, genetic engineering, cybernetics, nanotechnologies, and innumerable military technological advances, to name a few. It is a brave new world! But for most people, it is the same old one, when one faces the realities of economic inequalities and power struggles that have only increased and spread.

However, it would seem fair to expect that, once the "terror of a nuclear power equilibrium" (created by the United States and the Soviet Union to which the world was subjected during the last half of the 20th century) was overcome, the world could or should have evolved into a new age of understanding and harmony, which could have been achieved by female leaders. We should have experienced a renaissance on our planet, devoid of all empires. The American excuse for imperialistic behavior, needing to counterbalance the communist menace, had been eliminated. In its place, however, the gestation of a new excuse for imperialism had begun—the birth of the Multinational Corporation (MNC). This new kind of empire has neither geographical boundaries nor a national gravity center. Some believe that the governments of all the different countries (including those of the nuclear superpowers that were until recently in confrontation) should act as their foremen to help run the new empire.

The most formidable resource that this new empire appears to be relying upon is property rights for the ever-developing hard and soft technologies available. They are counting on having total dominion over the creation and dissemination of this technology so as to have dominion over the entire population of our planet. Its best ally, then, is the world-wide patent and trademark system and IPRs in general. Do we really want such a patent system which grossly over-rewards the few while depriving the many? In the year 2010, relatively global, harmonized, legislation dealing with IPRs should have been implemented, as the result of the Trade-Related Intellectual Property Rights (TRIPs) Agreement enforced by the World Trade Organization for all of its members. This re-hauled global legislation on IPRs will become, one could argue, the multinational's best ally, because these corporations are the ones that invest more in scientific and technological research and development (R&D). They are also the ones that most frequently appropriate the technological resources and creations that come from official institutions, such as state laboratories and other centers of research and universities. The individual and independent inventors and the small to medium-sized but innovative industries (for whom the original patent system was mainly developed) are becoming an extinct species.

Most inventors and innovators now either work on contract for these big centers of research, a priori, or end up selling their creations posteriori, because of lack of financial and technical capacity to develop them and/or to market them, even for lack of capacity to patent them. Patenting an invention world-wide with secure protection or real effective claim can cost hundreds of thousands of dollars. Therefore, they negotiate their creations and inventions to the corporations so that the big companies and the multinationals can exploit them "monopolistically" (with technological exclusivity) in the now globalized market of free trade and free competition. We are not trying to be ironic here, but to understand the context.

The conventional wisdom (and still very much valid presumption or argument in support of patents) is that the inventor or his employer shall enjoy the exclusivity rights to the exploitation of his creation, as an incentive and not as a compensation or reward for his effort and genius of creation, as many wrongly assume. These exclusivity rights are supposedly an incentive for the competition that is expected among all would-be and potential inventors so that they will then benefit society at large by continuously providing new and improved creations in the "useful arts" and technologies, per se. The exclusivity is actually much more of bait than a prize. Although it is really just a transitory property, it has been perceived, ever since, as a monopolistic right on his/her technology, and is still promoted and assumed, as such, by many.

After a period of exclusivity for this property (during such time when he/she decides who may or may not economically exploit his creation), his/her patent expires, and the technology reverts to the public domain (common property for all) as a part of humanity's common technological "stock" (heap) of property. The transitory element of this property has been established so that the exercise of this "apparent" monopoly should not collide with the sacred, supreme principle of free access and competition of free-market capitalism. It becomes then legitimated within the logic of the competition paradigm, now more important than ever, since the invigorated rhetoric of the principles of liberal free market and free trade are being promoted or pretended with the enforcement of globalization.

This formidable soft technology of IPRs is kept and legitimated, expanded and enforced by assisting and "persuading" third world or developing countries (second world countries, too), so that they will make it work efficiently by improving their legislation, their judicial systems, and the patents, copyrights, and trademark offices for the valid and effective enforcement and protection of the exclusive marketing and exploitation of goods related to these IPR's. In the meantime, such countries are denied the right to establish other protections or exclusivities ("barriers") for their own markets. Confusing and comparing IPR protection with the pervasive "protectionism," which is so much denounced and combated when dismantling barriers (especially custom-tariffs that protect incompetent and inefficient local producers) in favor of the free-trade doctrine would be an unfair and misleading oversight or simplification for sure. It takes expert knowledge not to do so in this situation. However, the confusion is going to occur or arise in several aspects, as we shall see later.

Nevertheless, one of the real, unfair oversights which seems to be taking place among the experts who are enforcing the validity, legitimacy, and effectiveness of the soft-technology being enforced (IPR's) is that this technology has pitfalls, contradictions, and obsoleteness with respect to today's world circumstances. The one that should be the most conspicuous of them all (with respect to the situation of the third world) is perhaps the one related precisely to the legitimacy of the patent's exclusive right to exploitation of technology sustained in the temporality of such exclusivity as not significantly diminishing (or even completely eroding) the free and fair competition that globalization is pretending. Since it is so ignored (consciously or not), it would seem that this pitfall and contradiction being overlooked requires specific explanation. As previously stated, the exclusive right of the inventor (in legal terms: the right to exclude others from the industrial or commercial exploitation of the technology) is justified in that this is what provides the incentive for potential creators and developers of technology to incur the extra costs and risks that innovating implies and, therefore, creating by such incentive—besides the new technologies—a new kind of layer of competition for the creation of technology in general. This last part is what most people who are acquainted with patents and IPRs seems to ignore.

In order not to convert this incentive into a real monopoly or an excess of incentive or privilege (in other words, to maintain or recover market competition at large) the conventional wisdom was that such exclusivity was meant to be temporary. After a certain time, others would be able to use and exploit said technology from then on, for the patent has expired. What is then being grossly overlooked is that this conventional wisdom has become mostly obsolete, since for most types of today's technologies, by the time the patent expires, the technology has long since become obsolete, out of competition in the market. That is to say, it has lost all competitive value in the everyday competitive market, especially because of the globalization rhetoric and reality of which we have been speaking. In much less than twenty years (the now universal time validity of the exclusive rights of patents, since TRIPs) the patented technology will have been already displaced and substituted by a totally new or improved technology which has most likely also been patented, and this will be the one technology capable of efficiently "competing" in the "free-trade" fully-globalized market place!

Therefore, we are bound to have a chained relay of exclusively-own technologies ("monopolies") in a world supposedly globalized, with the rhetoric of the benefits of free competition and free trade. In such a world, the less-developed countries are much more likely to remain in the conditions of being permanently net-importers and dependent on the first-world, privately-owned technology, and not creators of technology, since the high cost and complexity of creating competitive technology puts them at an immense disadvantage (although not impossibility) to compete for its creation. Do we see here the need for, among other measures, a non-exclusive patent-protection alternative? Should not the less-developed countries have the right to claim a different treatment in this respect? All TRIPs (WTO) gave them was a grace period of a maximum of five to ten years to comply with these agreements. What is ten years when the relative difference of technological and institutional development between these two worlds can be measured even in centuries? To add insult to injury, third-world countries have never been compensated for centuries of exploitation at the hands of the economically rewarded first-world countries. Nor have the cultural, institutional, and economic structures of disadvantages inherited from the period of colonization ever been sufficiently overcome in most cases.

A minimum base of institutional and organizational technology is needed for proper development and even for developing the capacity to create and compete in creating material technology. However, this last one (material) is much easier to be imported, consumed, copied, and utilized. The difference is that institutional (organizational) technologies, in order to work efficiently or effectively, depend upon values and beliefs, while material technologies depend upon knowledge. Knowledge is relatively easy to transmit or to copy—even to be changed—when compared with values and beliefs, especially institutional values that sometimes even collide with the legitimate values of those countries' particular histories, legal systems, and idiosyncrasies.

The goods of material technology (machinery, household appliances, and consumer goods in general) can very easily be imported and consumed or learned to be manufactured. But the minimum standards of institutional technologies that are needed for "proper" development cannot be imported, much less developing the capacity to create and "to compete" in creating material technology (which is the underlying rationality motivating the patent system in the first place). As stated above, we need to work towards creating a new layer of competition so that a two-way exchange of technology-value-added goods between both Worlds can then occur. Is this not what is pretended in the long run between both worlds? Or is there a double standard going on here? (See why the rhetoric about imperialism comes up?)

Nevertheless, the institutional paradigm is being enforced, since it cannot simply be imported but has to be valued and understood socially and politically, in order for the proper policies of investments and incentives in creating and competing for material technology to occur. This is where the real disadvantages of third-world countries (and probably second-world in some aspects) lie. If one adds to this scenario that these countries have very small or nonexistent budgets for research and development (R&D) it is only logical and understandable that they should demand a different approach to the IPR's enforced on them. This statement does not defend any kind of paternalistic approach as an alternative. The third world cannot afford the "brain drain" phenomenon which only creates a larger gap between the first and third worlds. This phenomenon will only make it impossible to achieve an equal, interdependent relationship, instead of continuing to propagate the status quo system of one-way dependency.

Now more than ever, traditional cultures are trying to adapt and keep up with the other modern, technological, and quickly-changing societies. Globalization is forcing many people to swim or sink as individuals and as cultures. So far, the most developed and technologically-advanced countries are deciding (in a very authoritarian, paternalistic way) the direction that the rest of the world should take. As in the past, some cultures are passively accepting this domineering behavior. However, some countries are refusing to be redefined by dominant ones.

Globalization in the hands of moral political and economic leaders could be the engine for rapid and positive change. The operative word for this theory to become a reality is "cooperation." It is possible that if we humans work together as a team, we could solve most of our global problems. Once in a while, when tragedies (like Hurricane Katrina or the earthquake in Haiti) afflict the people of one nation, we can see the potential for the global community to work together to help each other. Unfortunately, it takes a major tragedy for us to prioritize what should be the goal of global interdependency—to cooperate with each other for the benefit of humanity.

The rapid changes produced by modern technology require cooperation and fair treatment among nations. Intellectual property rights (IPRs) is just one of the many areas in which the powerful, developed nations can either help or break the poor, developing ones. An analogy that illustrates this practice is the competition presented to small businesses by giants like Wal-Mart. As a small, local business, it is impossible to survive and/or compete with the capital, resources, and international control of production and markets that global companies like Wal-Mart have at their disposal. The same applies to small countries that have to compete with countries like the U.S. and China. Only by implementing a fair and competitive international economic system will we see global stability and progress. In order to achieve this type of international, cooperative system, we will have to elect responsible and moral leaders who will be willing to stop the abuses and corruption of our present system. It comes down to priorities. From a historical point of view, male's priorities have been power, control, expansion, and subjugation. From the female's point of view, we could argue that the priorities would become human welfare, cooperation, and taking care of the most basic human needs.

Nationalism

> "Our times demand a new definition of leadership—global leadership. They demand a new constellation of international cooperation—governments, civil society and the private sector, working together for a collective global good."
>
> U.N. Secretary-General Ban Ki-Moon[106]

One of the most controversial and conflicting concepts developed by man is the concept of nationalism. The creation of nation-states, national identity, and the geographical divisions on the planet have resulted in a number of problems that have contributed to the reasons for war. The 20th century was witness to the only two world wars in history and an increasing amount of conflict and competition between nations. In a modern, technological world, economic, political, social, and cultural competition is being decided in Darwinian fashion. In other words, the technologically advanced nations threaten the survival of the less developed nations.

The idea of nation-building that has become part of the foreign policy of countries, such as the United States and Russia, has increased the number of conflicts within nation-states that do not want to be political and/or cultural colonies of the super-powers. It is ironic that those in the U.S. who ascribe to the conservative political ideology demand less government intervention and more local control at home but at the same time attempt to impose strong, centralized governments upon countries like Iraq and Afghanistan. The nation-building formula designed to control and artificially unify the people in those countries is a formula that historically is condemned to failure. The corrupt and power-hungry Iraqi politicians, different religious sects in the country, various political philosophies, and the linguistic and cultural differences found in Iraq are not conducive to the peaceful, tolerant environment necessary to achieve a modern, civilized society.

In the United States, one of the most pluralistic societies in the world, the problem of cultural identity represents a tremendous challenge for the new generations. As clearly explained by Samuel Huntington:

> "Some Americans have promoted multiculturalism at home; some have promoted universalism abroad; and some have done both. Multiculturalism at home threatens the United States and the West; universalism abroad threatens the West and the world. Both deny the uniqueness of Western culture . . . The global monoculturalists want to make the world like America. The domestic multiculturalists want to make America like the world. A multicultural America is impossible

because a non-Western America is not American. A multicultural world is unavoidable because global empire is impossible. The preservation of the United States requires renewal of Western identity. The security of the world requires acceptance of global multiculturality."[107]

If a super power, such as the U.S., truly wanted to help influence the development of developing nations like Iraq, it would have to influence by example, not by force. Historically, the imposition of values and institutions by force has been mainly a product of male authoritarian concepts. These values should be replaced by a nurturing and tolerant feminine approach. When the rest of the world sees that the U.S. has achieved the ideals of a harmonious, tolerant society and the majority of its citizens actively participate in the democratic process to elect moral and responsible leaders, only then will the rest of the world willingly follow the leadership of the United States and try to replicate its conduct.

Irrational, traditional, male behavior is exemplified by the decision of President Barack Obama to continue military occupation in Iraq and Afghanistan in the name of U.S. national security. The policy of withdrawing troops from Iraq in order to send them to Afghanistan did not fix the problem that plagues the people of those countries. They still live in the middle of a military occupation. Nor does this policy fix the dilemma of the innocent American soldiers who are being forced to fight a war for male political egos and private business interests. "National Security" is a concept used by most nations as an excuse to justify the very lucrative (for the people in power and their friends) business of war. The interconnection between the oil industry and the weapons industry is nothing but obscene. The sad reality is that the petro-dollars that countries, such as the U.S., spends on buying oil from OPEC countries, like Saud-Arabia, are spent in return by the Saudis to buy weapons from the U.S. In this process, the political and economic leaders of both nations become more powerful and wealthy. When we multiply the number of weapons sold, by the number of nations, by the number of corrupt leaders, we can easily see the tremendous amount of resources that are being wasted worldwide. Historically, when governments have domestic problems (usually because of incompetent or corrupt administrations), they often use the guise of national security or create an international conflict of some sort as a distraction and an attempt to get support from the people. By creating or exaggerating potential threats from other nations, these disingenuous leaders manipulate the masses in the name of patriotism.

In addition to searching for and placing moral leaders in power, along with educating the people on global issues, global understanding could be immensely improved if universities throughout the world sponsored international debates. By using modern technology, these debates could be televised worldwide so that citizens everywhere could listen to and understand what other people, especially the ones whom they consider enemies, have to say. Nations, political ideologies, religions, ethnic groups, scientists, etc. could have an international forum to present and defend their ideas, making room for honest, respectful and intellectual debates. Countries, organizations, and individuals could express their views by having their most eloquent minds representing them. Many leaders promote democratic values but forget to include in the equation for democracy the element of education. For the people to vote or choose between ideas or leaders without knowledge is a fallacy that gives people a false sense of participation. Many political and religious leaders would find excuses to avoid these international debates because their weaknesses and crimes would be revealed. On the other hand, the leaders and nations that have nothing to hide or manipulate would be open to debate.

Billions of people watch soccer games during the World Cup competition, and most recognize the stronger teams, not because they might be from prominent nations, but because those nations' players and coaches have worked harder or have developed better tactics. Likewise, the world is ready to have a global debate about the most controversial and urgent topics affecting the present or near future of the majority of the people on the planet. Topics such as war, poverty, energy, hunger, overpopulation, pollution, human rights, education, global warming, slavery, drug abuse, crime, immigration, and others should be discussed and debated in an open, international forum. The common goal of the debate would be to create mutual understanding, with the idea of working on compromises and applicable solutions without having a winner or loser, but rather an opportunity for each side to explain and present its ideas.

A case in point can be illustrated by a debate that could occur between the most eloquent representative of a socialist South American country and the most eloquent representative of the capitalist United States of America. If the people from both sides took the time to listen, it is possible that many of the misunderstandings and misconceptions that the people have would be eliminated. Let us have the debates at governmental, university, and high school levels in order not only to hear the most likely propagandistic version of the government, but also intellectual and inter-generational points of view. In order to make the debate more genuine, it could be followed by a second debate in which the facts (statistics) presented in the first debate could be confirmed or denied by independent international committees and exposed prior to the second debate. The idea is to avoid using misinformation from either side in order to make a point. For the first time in human history, we, the people, could communicate with each other in real time and find common ground without the corrupt manipulation of most governments. Television could be one of the most useful tools that humans have ever invented, if only we put it to work to educate the citizens of the world on the potential to achieve peace and prosperity for everyone. Let the debates begin!

At a national level, let us use the example of immigration for our chosen topic of discussion/debate. In order to understand the complexity of immigration, the process of migrating legally to the United States should be explained. Historically, people have migrated looking for a better place to live and raise a family. The United States of America is a nation of immigrants who have come from all over the world, but those immigrants have been predominantly of Western European descent. The famous poem by Emma Lazarus that appears at the base of the Statue of Liberty in the New York City harbor ("Give me your tired, your poor, your huddled masses yearning to breathe free . . .") has been an inspirational and exemplary symbol that has made this country one of the most advanced societies in history from a humanitarian perspective. For centuries people have been attracted by the greatest invitation of all time, "The New Colossus," written in 1883:

> **Not like the brazen giant of Greek fame,**
> **With conquering limbs astride from land to land;**
> **Here at our sea-washed, sunset gates shall stand**
> **A mighty woman with a torch, whose flame**
> **Is the imprisoned lightning, and her name,**
> **Mother of Exiles. From her beacon-hand**
> **Glows world-wide welcome; her mild eyes command**
> **The air-bridged harbor that twin cities frame.**
> **'Keep, ancient lands, your storied pomp!' cries she**
> **With silent lips. 'Give me your tired, your poor,**
> **Your huddled masses yearning to breathe free,**
> **The wretched refuse of your teeming shore.**
> **Send these, the homeless, tempest-tossed to me,**
> **I lift my lamp beside the golden door!'**

The Statue of Liberty was originally called "Liberty Enlightening the World." The problem is that this invitation no longer appears valid, due to the immigration policies of the last half-century. In order to be legally permitted to enter the United States of America, an individual cannot be poor. If you want to come as a tourist, you must have the economic means to travel and have a substantial amount of money in your bank account to be eligible for a visitor's visa. If you want to come to live permanently in the U.S., the requisites are so many and so difficult to achieve that a regular, middle-class citizen from most parts of the world would not qualify, let alone anyone with economic hardship. So when people say that anyone who wants to come to the United States should simply go to the American consulate and apply to migrate legally, they should investigate all that is required to obtain a visa, prior to stating that legal immigration is such a simple option.

The average potential immigrant earns less than $100 per month (which is often the motivation for migration). But the requirements to migrate legally are as listed:

1. A $470 non-refundable application fee (more than four months' salary)
2. Substantial funds in a savings account
3. A sponsor (relative already a legal citizen of the United States) with an income of at least 125% of the poverty line or $18,212 for a household of 2 as of 2010.
4. No sponsor, no visa, most likely
5. Even after all of these requirements are met, it usually takes five to ten years before legal migration status is approved.

It is clear that for the poor, the doors are closed. The vision of the United States for the poor is no longer that of the welcoming symbol of freedom that is the Statue of Liberty, but rather an exclusive and isolationist symbol that is the fortified U.S.-Mexican border. There is no way that any of these economically-challenged, U.S. hopefuls could afford even the migration application fee. Unfortunately, the majority of the people who try to justify their position against immigrants are ignorant of the legal process and requirements of legal migration.

Here is a good question: What would you do if you knew that you and your family could be much better off with an abundance of opportunities for your children simply by relocating to a city that happens to be another country? As a predominantly Christian nation, from the moral point of view, the question should be: What would Jesus Christ do about immigration? Would He stop people from going to a place where they could have a better life? Would He make it illegal for them to make the attempt at a new life, or would He welcome them and help them to achieve their goals? We know what the answers should be, but we will find excuses in order to rationalize the hypocritical way that we are dealing with the issue of immigration.

The problem of immigration is an international phenomenon that exists on every continent and will continue to exist as long as we cannot find pragmatic solutions to the problems of hunger, unemployment, wars, and oppression. Economic, political, and ecological realities dictate the need for people to migrate from one country to another. Only a comprehensive global approach to deal with the roots of the problem will allow the international community to live in an organized, harmonious world. Using common logic, we can see the pattern of immigration from poorer to richer countries with exponential complications. Under normal circumstances, Haitians (some of the poorest people on the planet) have been migrating to the Dominican Republic (with a less poor population) for decades, especially after the infamous earthquake that devastated Port au Prince and its proximal areas in January 2010. In the meantime, Dominicans have being migrating to the United States of America (a much wealthier country) to improve their standard of living. As more Haitians go to the Dominican Republic and compete for scarce jobs and resources, more Dominicans and Haitians attempt to migrate by any means possible to what is still seen as the "land of opportunity."

As stated several times in this book, a logical, pragmatic solution to many of the world's problems would be to stop wasting limited resources on weapons and military-related expenditures and to, instead, use those resources to create jobs, educate people, and attempt to eliminate hunger. For the most part, people will stay in their native countries, cities, and regions close to their friends and families if they have a decent standard of living. Unfortunately, for most people living in the present, male-dominated, militaristic world, the chances for real positive change are miniscule. The real change has to be a change in paradigms where (as was explained previously) female leaders, with their more nurturing nature, would trade the sword for the plow, the tanks for the schools, and aircraft carriers for hospitals. With modern agricultural technology, there is no excuse for the fact that in the 21st century millions of people die of hunger and malnutrition. The essence of the problem is that because of ignorance and cultural inertia, we allow the pre-historic, male-oriented society to continue to dominate our lives. We have solutions to most of the problems confronting humanity; we just lack the leaders and the will to implement them.

Chapter 9

Social Evolution

For thousands of years, religions have tried to create a culture of love, peace, and harmony; unfortunately, it appears that humans have ignored the messages of religion and have immersed themselves in a culture of envy and conflict. This envy has been founded and produced by the contrast between opulence and misery. It has been founded upon the chasm between consumerism and scarcity. Frequently, we in the United States are inclined to become the envy of others in less fortunate areas of the world. Furthermore, our culture encourages us to become the world's ultimate consumers, exacerbating the great divide between the "haves" and "have-nots." Many segments of publicity, such as the news, literature, television and radio programming bombard us daily with information designed to manipulate us into buying more. When a manufacturer or salesperson of a product wants to promote or express the quality of his products, he presents the superiority of his product in comparison to the competition. Commercial propaganda presents a "cult of exclusivity" which appeals to the same emotional substance of which envy is made. Frequently, people are not capable of enjoying their well-being, if it is not envied by others.

We all know the person whose goal is to purchase only exclusive brand items so that he can be envied by fellow members of our materialistic culture. We all know the student whose goal is not to get good grades, but rather to be envied by his classmates for his good grades. We know men who do not enjoy their beautiful companions or "conquests" unless they can show off their "trophy" women to other males who will then envy them. Owners of luxury cars want to be envied by owners of more modest vehicles, and so on and so forth. Included in this group are parents who revel in the envy of other parents over the accomplishments of their offspring. We have created a society and civilization where it is impossible to measure how much damage, unhappiness, limitations, and frustrations we have caused because we have allowed ourselves to be victims or instruments of envy. If the supporters of the Marxist dialectic ("From each, according to his abilities; to each, according to his needs") had included in their categories the study of envy and the relationships that this emotion generates, they probably could have achieved a more successful and revolutionary paradigm than Marx's famous (and eventually discredited) statement.

When speaking of dialectics, dualities, and contradictions, what is the emotion contrary to envy? Scholars of knowledge have established the principal of duality as a universal one. Therefore, each concept is associated or contrasted with its antonym. In biological terms, we have males and females; in psychological terms, we have masculine and feminine. All of the cognitive or emotional dimensions appear to have this dual characterization. The world of ethics is polarized between good and bad, right and wrong, virtues and vices. In the case of aesthetics, there is beauty and ugliness, the wonderful and the horrible. In terms of senses, there is dark and light, hard and soft, hot and cold, sweet and sour, rough and smooth, etc. Emotional terms have synthesized within them all of the above dualities and categories. The typical ones are love and hate, sublime and vulgar, happy and sad, valor and cowardice, altruism and egoism, and many more.

This emotional realm of terms is precisely where there should exist a feeling opposite to envy. What is this opposite to envy and what do we call it? Frequently people's answers are sympathy or generosity. Nevertheless, we could explain that the contrary to generosity is greed and the contrary of sympathy is antipathy. None of these feelings represent the duality or the contraposition of envy. It could possibly be associated in another form. The dictionary defines envy as a feeling of discontent or covetousness with regard to another's advantages, success, possessions, etc. The Catholic catechism teaches that there are seven capital sins, so it wisely proposed charity as a resource against envy. However, charity is not really the antonym of envy. Even though it promotes condolence for other people's sorrows, it does not guarantee happiness or general well-being. The existence of an antonym of envy has been a challenge even for polyglots to determine if the word exists in another language. So far there has not been an adequate word found that contains, in semantic terms, the precision of a true antonym to the concept of envy, the way so many other dualities have been paired. It is as the dictionaries express. Envy is a negative feeling of being bothered or of the sadness that is produced by viewing the pleasure or well-being of others. Its contrary should be a positive feeling of happy satisfaction for any improvement in the situation of others.

What is more foreign or unnatural for us is to feel unhappiness caused by the well-being of others. If instead of feeling envious of someone else we could feel happiness for the good things that happen to others, we would be feeling the opposite of envy. We would then be feeling _____ (happy for you)? There is no word for it. If you thought about empathy, remember that empathy is the affinity or identification for what someone else is feeling. It could be his or her happiness or sadness. Besides, you cannot feel empathy for something that someone else has. In most cases envy is caused by the desire for the material goods that others have, without even knowing for sure what that person feels about having those goods. Therefore, the word for the opposite of envy should include the satisfaction and happiness produced in us by seeing the material goods and success that others have, and our good wishes for their welfare.

Some believe that the feeling contrary to envy can only be exemplified by the feelings we have toward our loved ones. When our loved ones, such as our children, possess an object or characteristic that may make others envious, we, the parents of those children, usually feel great joy and satisfaction. Perhaps it is a matter of having a vicarious experience through our children, thereby eliminating the envy that we might otherwise feel. Envy, on the other hand, is caused by the sight of the welfare and well-being of strangers, and sometimes even our friends and loved ones. Why can't people feel the contrary of envy for the welfare of strangers? Some would argue that this feeling does not exist, and that the contrary of envy can be understood as the pleasure or enjoyment that we feel for the suffering and/or problems and misery of others. This perverse feeling is the sadistic contrary of compassion or charity. Is it possible that the opposite feeling of envy is so rare that our cultures have not identified it, yet, so that there has not risen a necessity to name this feeling?

This dilemma seems to present a grotesque and asymmetric duality. Envy is a very old word for which people have not even felt the need to label its scarce partner in the duality. If the dialectic indicates a cognitive sequence in its dynamic of thesis, antithesis, and then synthesis that becomes the thesis again in a new cognitive scale or platform, we would have to ask ourselves if the sequence of this duality in relation to envy is still at the stage preponderant to the thesis, if it lacks an antithesis. Could it be that the evolutionary state of the human species is morally and/or emotionally so underdeveloped and primitive that it has not identified the opposite feeling of envy? If we have already conceptualized it, can we just baptize it, promote it, poeticize it, sublimate it, and more importantly teach it? Having developed the definition of the feeling (essentially maternal instinct) that is contrary to envy, (many have probably felt it even though they've never named it) let us invent a name for it. After all, every word was invented by someone at one point in time. Why can we not invent this word in question? If we are talking about a very infrequent or very scarce feeling, then maybe with the magic of words we could legitimate and propagate it. With the baptism of this new concept we could promote it, make it strong, and, with it, combat envy. As Doroteo Rodriguez proposes, "With the hope that many synonyms will emerge, let's name it alegrotria/allegrotry: 'sentimiento de alegria or satisfaccion causado por la felicidad o el bien ajeno o de otros, antonimo de la envidia,' (a feeling of happiness or goodwill caused by the well-being and joy of others, an antonym of envy.)"[108]

Even though many religious institutions preach the idea of universal love, unfortunately, it usually ends up being part of the once-a-week, usual, religious lesson, rather than being genuinely practiced in daily life toward our fellow human beings. If instead of talking about loving each other, we talk about the actual actions of love (giving, sharing, and caring in church, school, work, and life), the world would be much better off. Imagine that a young mind can learn anything bad, including the extreme examples of children who become suicide bombers by learning fanatical concepts that should be completely foreign and irrational to any sane mind by nature. What extreme opposites, then, could be instilled in the minds of children? What extreme versions of love, compassion, and forgiveness could be taught? The most important part to creating a better society is the famous concept of teaching by example. It does not make much sense to preach one thing and do something else. Hypocrisy is one of the major reasons that modern society is in such shambles. The French philosopher Teilhard de Charden reinterpreted many disciplines, including theology, sociology, and metaphysics, around this understanding of the universe. His main focus was to reassure the converging mass of humanity not to despair, but to trust the evolution of consciousness as it rises through them.

As we have stated throughout this book, by selecting the positive and humanitarian aspects from all religious, political, social, and economic systems, and by using a universal education system, we could finally move toward a more just, peaceful, feminine, and humanitarian world.

Conclusion

In the words of Peter Berger: "The history of mankind is a history of pain. The pain inflicted by nature usually appears in the historical records only in its most spectacular manifestations . . . But the pain inflicted by men on each other is the indispensable raw material of the historian's reconstructions. Looking backward from the vantage point of the present, history appears as an endless series of massacres."[109]

Many experts in international relations, politics, sociology, and related academic fields tend to believe that the 21st century will see an increase in economic, political, and social problems, and that our present organizational structures are handicapped in their efforts to improve our human plight. On the contrary, we strongly believe that real, positive, vital changes can finally be achieved by exchanging traditional, male-dominated organizational and social structures with a progressive and creative female paradigm. However, we also believe that the pessimistic view of the future role of Western Culture (dominated by the U.S.) as discussed by the German philosopher, Oswald Spengler,[110] in his book, *The Decline of the West*, may also be true, especially if the West continues along its entropic path of male-dominated, aggressive, militaristic leadership.

In a male-dominated world, fortitude and leadership are often confused with aggressiveness, belligerence, and stubbornness. It is easy to appear to be a tough, strong leader when that leader can easily send others into harm's way to do his fighting for him. In modern conflicts, political leaders are never generals who must lead their soldiers into battle, as they did in the past. Remaining "cozy in the castle," while their "chess pawns" put their lives on the line, makes it easy for these "leaders" to waste manpower on destructive pursuits. Today's battles require, instead, leaders who have the courage to fight for their principles and moral convictions, battling powerful economic and political interest groups who, for the most part, are motivated by greed and male egos, hungry for power and money.

Unlike Spengler, who believed that the West was heading into its Winter (decline) and would eventually be replaced by other civilizations, we believe that the West (especially the United States of America) has the potential to reshape and revolutionize the future of humanity by utilizing the wisdom, intellect, creativity, and nurturing capacity of females to manifest a New World Order based upon The Golden Rule—Do Unto Others as You Would Have Others Do Unto You. A greater philosophy to direct the behavior of humankind has never been spoken.

We have had many revolutions, from the industrial revolution to improve productivity, to the green revolution to multiply the amount of food we produce, to the computer revolution to increase computational and communications abilities. What we need now more than ever is the human/educational revolution in which the full human potential can be achieved. It is time for motherhood (the most powerful of human emotions) and noble female attributes to be the architects of our social, political, and economic institutions. Education is the tool that will revolutionize what we call mankind into a higher level of human development that we could call "womankind." Indeed, the Female Paradigm is truly an idea whose time has come.

Bibliography

NOTES

1. Zalben, Jane Breskin. *Paths to Peace: People Who Changed the World*. New York: Dutton Juvenile, 2006. Print.

2. Herbert, Bob. "Politics and Misogyny—New York Times." *The New York Times* . N.p., 15 Jan. 2008. Web. 30 Oct. 2010.

3. Mead, Margaret. *Male and Female*. 1 ed. New York: Harper Perennial, 2001. Print.

4. Toffler, Alvin. *Future Shock*. New York: Random House, 1970. Print.

5. Burton, Robert. *The mating game* . New York: Crown, 1976. Print.

6. Darwin, Charles. *The Origin Of Species*. New York: Signet Classics, 2003. Print.

7. Goldberg, P. "Are Women Prejudiced Against Women." *Transaction* April (1968): 28-33. Print.

8. Weiss, Paul. *Sport; a philosophic inquiry*. Carbondale: Southern Illinois University Press, 1969. Print.

9. Riencourt, Amaury De. *Sex and Power in History*. Philidalphia: New York: Mckay, 1974. Print.

10. Jeanniere, Abel. *The Anthropology of Sex*. New York: Harper And Row, 1964. Print.

11. Riencourt, Amaury De. *Sex and Power in History*. Philidalphia: New York: Mckay, 1974. Print.

12. Singer, June. *Androgyny: Toward a New Theory of Sexuality*. 1st ed ed. New York: Doubleday, 1976. Print.

13. Myers, David G. *Social Psychology*. 9th ed. Boston: Mcgraw-Hill College, 2007. Print.

14. Hosoda, Megumi. "Current Gender Stereotypes and their evaluative content." *Perceptual And Motor Skills* 90 (2000): 1283-1294. Print.

15. Mead, Margaret. *Male and Female*. 1 ed. New York: Harper Perennial, 2001. Print.

16. Peck, Translator. Aristotle. A. L. *Generation of Animals*. null. Reprint. New York: Harvard, 1963. Print.

17. D'Andrade, R. *The Development of Sex Differences*. 1St Edition ed. Stanford, California: Stanford Univ Pr, 1966. Print.

18. Hayes, Thomas David Boslooper; Marcia. *THE FEMININITY GAME*. First Edition ed. New York: Stein And Day, 1973. Print.

19. Bem, Sandra. "Sex Typing and the Avoidance of Cross-sex Behavior." *Journal of Personality and Social Psychology* 33 (1976): 48-54. Print.

20. Sherman, J.A. "Social Values, Femininity and the Development of Female Competence." *Journal of Social Issues,* 32 (1976): 59-66. Print.

21. Pandey, Kundan. "Strong Women Quotes." *Buzzle Web Portal: Intelligent Life on the Web*. N.p., n.d. Web. 1 Mar. 2011. <http://www.buzzle.com/articles/strong-women-quotes.html>.

22. Frieze, I.H. "Nonverbal Maintence of Traditional Sex-Roles." *Journal of Social Issues* 32 (1976): 3-10. Print.

23. Maccoby, Eleanor E., and Carol Nagy Jacklin. *The psychology of sex differences*. London.: Oxford University Press, 1975. Print.

24. Kagan, J. "Aquisition and Significance of Sex Typing and Sex-Role Identity." *Review of child development research* 7 (1965): 61-68. Print.

25. Parlee, M.B. "Postpartum Depression." *Obstetrics and Gynecology* 1 (1975): 5-10. Print.

26. Hayes, Thomas David Boslooper; Marcia. *THE FEMININITY GAME*. First Edition ed. New York: Stein And Day, 1973. Print.

27. Wolf, W.C. "Sex and Authority in the Workplace: The Causes of Sexual Inequality." *American Sociological Review.* 4 (1979): 235-252. Print.

28. Duberman, Lucile. *Gender and Sex in Society*. Austin: Holt Rinehart & Winston, 1975. Print.

29. O'Barr, J. "Third World Women: Factors in Their Changing Status." *Center for International Studies* 2 (1976): 7-8. Print.

30. Hayes, Thomas David Boslooper; Marcia. *THE FEMININITY GAME*. First Edition ed. New York: Stein And Day, 1973. Print.

31. Sherman, J.A. "Social Values, Femininity and the Development of Female Competence." *Journal of Social Issues,* 32 (1976): 59-66. Print.

32. Bem, Sandra Lipsitz. *Bem inventory*. California: Consulting Psychologists Press, 1978. Print.

33. Bem, Sandra Lipsitz. *Bem inventory*. California: Consulting Psychologists Press, 1978. Print.

34. Jones, W.H. "The Enigma of Androgyny." *Journal of Counseling and Clinical Psychology* 46 (1978): 298-313. Print.

35. Spence, Janet. *Masculinity and Femininity: Their Psychological Dimensions, Correlates and Antecedents*. Austin: University of Texas Press, 1978. Print.

36. O'neil, James M. "Male Sex Role Conflicts, Sexism, and Masculinity: Psychological Implications for Men, Women, and the Counseling Psychologist ." *The Counseling Psychologist* 9.2 (1981): 61-80. Print.

37. Goffman, E. "Genderisims." *Psychology Today* II (1977): 60-63. Print.

38. Hart, M. "Women Sit at the Back of the Bus." *Psychology Today* October (1971): 63. Print.

39. Frieze, I.H. "Nonverbal Maintence of Traditional Sex-Roles." *Journal of Social Issues* 32 (1976): 3-10. Print.

40. Block, J. "Conceptions of Sex-Roles." *American Psychologist* 28 (1973): 512-526. Print.

41. Ridley, J. "Demographic Change and the Roles and Status of Women." *Annals of the American Academy of Political and Social Sciences* 375 (1968): 12. Print.

42. Spence, Janet. *Masculinity and Femininity: Their Psychological Dimensions, Correlates and Antecedents*. Austin: University of Texas Press, 1978. Print.

43. Hersh, Blanche. *SLAVERY OF SEX*. Urbana: University of Illinois Press, 1978. Print.

44. Lederer, William J., and Don D. Jackson. *The mirages of marriage,* . [1st ed. New York: W. W. Norton, 1968. Print.

45. Pandey, Kundan. "Strong Women Quotes." *Buzzle Web Portal: Intelligent Life on the Web*. N.p., n.d. Web. 1 Mar. 2011. <http://www.buzzle.com/articles/strong-women-quotes.html>.

46. Driessnack, John. "Racism, sexism still prevalent today despite what many think—CollegiateTimes.com." *Virginia Tech, Blacksburg & New River Valley News—CollegiateTimes.com*. N.p., n.d. Web. 7 Feb. 2011. <http://www.collegiatetimes.com/stories/14512/racism-sexism-still-prevalent-today-despite-what-many-think>.

47. O'neil, James M. "Male Sex Role Conflicts, Sexism, and Masculinity: Psychological Implications for Men, Women, and the Counseling Psychologist ." *The Counseling Psychologist* 9.2 (1981): 61-80. Print.

48. Wilson, Annie. *The wise virgin: The missing link between men and women*. New York: Turnstone Books, 1979. Print.

49. Bullough, Bonnie, and Vern L. Bullough. *The Subordinate Sex: A History of Attitudes Toward Women*. Urbana: University of Illinois Press, 1973. Print.

50. Stevens, E.P. "Machismo and Marianismo." *society* Sept/Oct (1973): 57-63. Print.

51. Williamson, Robert C., and Eds. Georgene H. Seward. *Sex Roles in Changing Society*. New York: Random House, 1970. Print.

52. Sau, Victoria. *Manifiesto Para La Liberacion De La Mujer*. Barcelona, EspaÃ±a: Editorial Bruguera, 1975. Print.

53. Ruether, Rosemary Radford. *New women, new earth: sexist ideologies and human liberation.* New York: The Seabury Press, 1975. Print.

54. Estudios, Andinos. "La Mujer Durante la Conquista y la Primera Epoca Colonial." *Estudios Andinos* 5.7 (1976): 1-36. Print.

55. Williamson, Robert C., and Eds. Georgene H. Seward. *Sex Roles in Changing Society.* New York: Random House, 1970. Print.

56. Garcia Lorca, Federico. *YERMA*. Madrid: Reysa Ediciones S.R.L., 2007. Print.

57. D'Andrade, R. *The Development of Sex Differences.* 1St Edition ed. Stanford, California: Stanford Univ Pr, 1966. Print.

58. Bullough, Bonnie, and Vern L. Bullough. *The Subordinate Sex: A History of Attitudes Toward Women.* Urbana: University of Illinois Press, 1973. Print.

59. H., M. Bacon, and I. Child. "A Cross-Cultural Survey of Some Sex Differences in Socialization." *Journal of Abnormal and Social Psychology* 55 (1957): 327-332. Print.

60. Goldberg, P. "Are Women Prejudiced Against Women." *Transaction* April (1968): 28-33. Print.

61. "TIME Cover Depicts the Disturbing Plight of Afghan Women—TIME." *Breaking News, Analysis, Politics, Blogs, News Photos, Video, Tech Reviews—TIME.com.* N.p., n.d. Web. 27 Jan. 2011. <http://www.time.com/time/world/article/0,8599,2007269,00.html>.

62. Maccoby, Eleanor E., and Carol Nagy Jacklin. *The psychology of sex differences* . London.: Oxford University Press, 1975. Print.

63. Orr, D.W. "Anthropological and Historical Notes on the Female Sexual Role." *Journal of the American psycho-Analytic Association* 6 (1968): 601-612. Print.

64. Ruether, Rosemary Radford. *New women, new earth: sexist ideologies and human liberation.* New York: The Seabury Press, 1975. Print.

65. Riencourt, Amaury De. *Sex and Power in History.* Philidalphia: New York: Mckay, 1974. Print.

66. Giele, Janet Zollinger, and Audrey C. Smock. *Women: roles and status in eight countries.* New York: Wiley, 1977. Print.

67. Bullough, Bonnie, and Vern L. Bullough. *The Subordinate Sex: A History of Attitudes Toward Women.* Urbana: University of Illinois Press, 1973. Print.

68. Russo, N.F. "The Motherhood Mandate." *Journal of Social Issues.* 32 (1976): 143-153. Print.

69. Mead, Margaret. *Male and Female.* 1 ed. New York: Harper Perennial, 2001. Print.

70. O'neil, James M. "Male Sex Role Conflicts, Sexism, and Masculinity: Psychological Implications for Men, Women, and the Counseling Psychologist ." *The Counseling Psychologist* 9.2 (1981): 61-80. Print.

71. Chasteen, Edgar R. *The case for compulsory birth control,.* New York: Prentice-Hall, 1971. Print.

72. O'Barr, J. "Third World Women: Factors in Their Changing Status." *Center for International Studies* 2 (1976): 7-8. Print.

73. O'Barr, J. "Third World Women: Factors in Their Changing Status." *Center for International Studies* 2 (1976): 7-8. Print.

74. Ridley, J. "Demographic Change and the Roles and Status of Women." *Annals of the American Academy of Political and Social Sciences* 375 (1968): 12. Print.

75. Bullough, Bonnie, and Vern L. Bullough. *The Subordinate Sex: A History of Attitudes Toward Women*. Urbana: University of Illinois Press, 1973. Print.

76. Jackson, M.D. William J. Lederer/Don D. *Mirages of Marriage*. New York: Norton, 1968. Print.

77. Pleck, J. "The Male Sex-Role:Definitions, Problems, and Sources of Change." The Journal of Social Issues. 32 (1976): 3. Print.

78. Rich, William. *Smaller families through social and economic progress* . Washington: Overseas Development Council, 1973. Print.

79. Bernard, Jessie. "The Status of Women in Modern Patterns of Culture." *The Annals of the American Academy of Political and Social Science* 375 (1968): 3-14. Print

80. Hoffman, Lois Wladis, and Martin L. Hoffman. *The value of children to parents* . Ann Arbor, Mich.: Department of Population Planning School of Public Health, University of Michigan, 1973. Print.

81. Veever, J.E. "the social meaning of parenthood." *Psychiatry* 36 (1973): 291-310. Print.

82. Bernard, Jessie. "The Status of Women in Modern Patterns of Culture." *The Annals of the American Academy of Political and Social Science* 375 (1968): 3-14. Print.

83. Lynn, David B. *Parental and sex-role identification*. Berkeley: McCutchan Pub. Corp., 1969. Print.

84. Bernard, Jessie. "Change and Stability in Sex-Role Norms and Behavior." *Journal of Social Issues* 32 (1976): 207-223. Print.

85. Ridley, J. "Demographic Change and the Roles and Status of Women." *Annals of the American Academy of Political and Social Sciences* 375 (1968): 12. Print.

86. Bernard, Jessie. "Change and Stability in Sex-Role Norms and Behavior." *Journal of Social Issues* 32 (1976): 207-223. Print.

87. Lederer, William J., and Don D. Jackson. *The mirages of marriage,* . [1st ed. New York: W. W. Norton, 1968. Print.

88. O'Barr, J. "Third World Women: Factors in Their Changing Status." *Center for International Studies* 2 (1976): 7-8. Print.

89. O'Barr, J. "Third World Women: Factors in Their Changing Status." *Center for International Studies* 2 (1976): 7-8. Print.

90. Peccei, Aurelio. *Human Quality.* Great Britain: Pergamon Pr, 1977. Print.

91. Toffler, Alvin. *Future Shock.* New York: Random House, 1970. Print.

92. Toffler, Alvin. *Future Shock.* New York: Random House, 1970. Print.

93. Walker, Gail. "United Nations Radio." *United Nations Multimedia, Radio, Photo and Television.* N.p., n.d. Web. 30 Oct. 2010.

94. Skidmore, Max J. *American political thought* . New York: St. Martin's Press, 1978.

95. Postman, Neil. *The End of Education: Redefining the Value of School.* null. Reprint. New York: Vintage, 1996. Print.

96. Harmer, Ruth Mulvey. *American medical avarice.* London: Abelard-Schuman, 1975. Print.

97. "ECHO :: Agricultural Resources." *ECHO :: Home.* N.p., n.d. Web. 27 Jan. 2011. <http://www.echonet.org/content/agriculturalResources>.

98. "He may be a son-of-a-bitch, but he is our son-of-a-bitch@Everything2.com." *Everything2.* N.p., n.d. Web. 5 Mar. 2011. <http://everything2.com/title/He+may+be+a+son-of-a-bitch%252C+but+he+is+our+son-of-a-bitch>.

99. "U.S.-Chile Documents." *The George Washington University.* N.p., n.d. Web. 27 Jan. 2011. <http://www.gwu.edu/~nsarchiv/NSAEBB/NSAEBB8/nsaebb8.htm>.

100. Hanson, Sigurd. "Peshawar Diary: 'Terror is Ugly. So is War'." *Analysis, Politics, Blogs, News Photos, Video, Tech Reviews—TIME. com.* N.p., n.d. Web. 30 Oct. 2010. <http://www.time.com/time/printout/0,8816,182352,00.html>.

101. Skidmore, Max J. *American political thought*. New York: St. Martin's Press, 1978.

102. Postman, Neil. *The End of Education: Redefining the Value of School.* null. Reprint. New York: Vintage, 1996. Print.

103. Carter, Jimmy. *Our Endangered Values: America's Moral Crisis.* New York, NY: Simon & Schuster, 2006. Print.

104. Carter, Jimmy. *The Blood of Abraham: Insights into the Middle East.* 3 ed. Fayetteville: University of Arkansas Press, 1993. Print.

105. Rodriguez Y., Doroteo A. "Inventions, patents and globalization." *WIPO/UNIVERSITY OF TORINO/ILO* 1.November (2000): 5-11. Print.

106. Ki-moon, Ban. "UN and Civil Society." *Welcome to the United Nations*. N.p., 29 Jan. 2009. Web. 30 Oct. 2010. <http://www.un.org/en/civilsociety/index.shtml>.

107. Huntington, Samuel P. *The Clash of Civilizations and the Remaking of World Order*. 1st Touchstone Ed ed. New York, NY: Simon & Schuster, 1998. Print.

108. Rodriguez, Doroteo A. "Alegrotria." *Listin Diario* [Santo Domingo] 5 Jan. 1993: 1. Print.

109. Berger, Peter L. *Pyramids of Sacrifice: Political Ethics and Social Change*. New York: Anchor, 1976. Print.

110. Spengler, Oswald, and Charles Francis Atkinson. *The decline of the West*. New York: A. A. Knopf, 1926. Print.

Index

A

Abigail Adams, 74
adulterers, 60
Afghanistan, 28, 64, 121, 128, 156, 157
African-American, 116
Africans, 112, 113, 114, 115
aggressive, 9, 10, 13, 20, 21, 33, 34, 38, 41, 42, 50, 53, 55, 56, 132, 135, 138, 141, 142, 169
agricultural, 58, 63, 66, 70, 94, 95, 99, 100, 101, 102, 128, 132, 162
altruism, 136, 165
American experiment, 43, 109, 121
American influence, 118
American leaders, 122, 123
American people, 16, 119, 120, 121, 122, 123, 126
Americans, 32, 50, 52, 54, 78, 86, 106, 118, 120, 134, 156
androgyny, 33, 41, 43
Anglo-Saxons, 112
Armaments, 130
arms, 64, 129
Asia, 106
attitudes, 31, 37, 46, 66, 68, 125

Augusto Pinochet, 118
authoritarian, 52, 70, 122, 123, 126, 140, 154, 157

B

bio-fuel, 98, 100, 101, 102
biological differences, 13, 29, 70
birth control, 9, 27, 29, 31, 57, 61, 68, 69, 72, 81, 96, 97, 98
birth rate, 96
blacks, 107, 108, 113, 114, 115
Bush administration, 79

C

candidates, 42, 86
capitalism, 90, 93, 143, 151
capitalist, 93, 131, 137, 148, 159
Caucasian, 72, 109, 111
Caucasians, 106, 111, 112
children, 21, 24, 30, 36, 40, 49, 50, 51, 52, 55, 57, 58, 60, 61, 62, 63, 65, 68, 70, 73, 75, 77, 83, 85, 91, 95, 96, 105, 110, 111, 129, 132, 135, 136, 137, 139, 142, 161, 166, 167, 168

Chile, 118, 119, 120
China, 121, 144, 155
Christian, 74, 86, 111, 134, 161
Christians, 134, 138
citizens, 10, 21, 65, 73, 74, 82, 85, 93, 96, 120, 122, 123, 127, 133, 134, 143, 157, 158, 159
Civil War, 32
civilization, 21, 31, 35, 54, 55, 56, 62, 70, 130, 143, 165
civilizations, 14, 35, 43, 68, 170
civilized, 17, 53, 65, 88, 130, 141, 142, 156
Cold War, 118, 125, 145
colonization, 76, 153
compassion, 7, 16, 19, 22, 43, 167, 168
competition, 10, 15, 17, 41, 93, 132, 143, 145, 146, 150, 151, 152, 153, 155, 156, 158, 164
conception, 31, 46, 59
Conflict Resolution, 87
Constitution, 86
contraception, 59
cooperation, 10, 17, 19, 21, 25, 41, 84, 85, 135, 139, 154, 155
corporations, 144, 145, 146, 149, 150
corruption, 76, 93, 126, 155
Costa Rica, 90
crime, 50, 59, 82, 97, 98, 109, 131, 159
crimes, 16, 77, 79, 88, 126, 130, 131, 132, 133, 158
criminals, 79, 88, 126, 132
cross-cultural, 13, 53, 54, 69, 84
Cuba, 118, 124
cultural difference, 109
cultural identities, 138
cultural programs, 132
culture, 16, 17, 22, 28, 31, 36, 43, 44, 47, 51, 52, 53, 54, 55, 60, 64, 69, 73, 76, 80, 90, 109, 110, 112, 117, 133, 135, 137, 142, 164
curriculum, 80, 83, 85, 87

D

Darwinian, 10, 17, 22, 24, 156
Declaration of Human Rights, 78
demagogue, 42
democracy, 10, 16, 23, 76, 84, 85, 93, 110, 116, 122, 123, 124, 130, 158
Democracy, 43, 122, 123
democratic elections, 85
democratic ideals, 118
demographic, 61, 63, 65
demographics, 95, 108
Denmark, 64, 73
dependency, 16, 37, 65, 69, 102, 103, 154
destruction, 13, 19, 77, 79, 83, 85, 95, 97, 99, 119, 122, 123, 125, 128, 129
determinism, 29, 66
developing countries, 28, 50, 53, 56, 61, 147, 151
developing nations, 61, 65, 143, 144, 157
dictatorial regimes, 118, 127
diplomacy, 121, 124, 130
disarmament, 15, 128

Disarmament, 130
discrimination, 40, 49, 50, 83, 86, 108, 141
divorce, 32, 45, 47, 52, 112
DNA testing, 75
doctors, 89, 90, 91
dominant, 34, 35, 37, 38, 40, 53, 71, 76, 145, 148, 154
Dominican Republic, 102, 118, 162
Doroteo Rodriguez, 143, 167
double standards, 41, 47, 60, 67, 68, 73, 83, 86, 88, 110, 130
duality, 73, 165, 167

E

ECHO, 94, 128
ecological, 10, 15, 61, 70, 99, 145, 162
economic development, 63, 67, 117, 143
economic institutions, 17, 170
economic interests, 140
economic problems, 95, 124
economic resources, 89
economic systems, 81, 168
education, 9, 10, 14, 15, 17, 19, 22, 23, 29, 31, 32, 33, 37, 44, 45, 47, 49, 51, 56, 59, 60, 61, 63, 64, 65, 66, 72, 73, 75, 76, 77, 80, 81, 82, 85, 91, 92, 93, 94, 95, 96, 97, 98, 103, 105, 108, 109, 110, 111, 112, 116, 121, 122, 123, 126, 128, 129, 131, 135, 136, 138, 139, 141, 142, 145, 158, 159, 168

Educational, 93, 128
educational experiences, 113, 114, 115
educational process, 86
educational resources, 97
educational value, 84
electricity, 103, 148
emancipated, 32
emotional toxicity, 132
emotionally-handicapped, 121
employment, 56, 57
energy, 10, 13, 15, 22, 80, 81, 97, 98, 99, 100, 101, 102, 103, 129, 145, 158
entropic nature, 15
entropy, 103
environment, 22, 51, 67, 74, 127, 135, 138, 156
environmental consequences, 80
environmental degradation, 100, 125
envy, 22, 121, 164, 165, 166, 167, 168
equality, 27, 28, 31, 35, 37, 40, 44, 49, 52, 57, 59, 62, 64, 69, 70, 74, 75, 86, 96, 110, 112, 116, 118, 122, 123
ethnic groups, 104, 108, 158
extremists, 54, 124, 125

F

family planning, 96, 98
fanatics, 36, 124
female leaders, 13, 17, 23, 99, 138, 149, 162
female paradigm, 15, 16, 169
Female Paradigm, 1, 3, 7, 11

feminine, 28, 33, 34, 41, 42, 43, 44, 51, 56, 86, 122, 123, 141, 157, 165, 168
femininity, 34, 35, 36, 41, 42, 43, 85
feminist, 46, 64
financial responsibilities, 92
first world, 34, 57, 97, 98
food, 15, 22, 30, 34, 55, 81, 92, 93, 94, 96, 102, 128, 131, 170
foreign policy, 86, 119, 120, 124, 156
foreign relations, 80, 122, 123
freedom, 16, 50, 56, 74, 86, 110, 117, 118, 122, 123, 138, 161
free-trade, 144, 145, 151, 152

G

Gandhi, 134
Garcia Lorca, 52
gender roles, 29, 31, 34, 43, 44, 55, 63, 65, 72
genetic engineering, 140, 148
geography, 80, 81, 107
geopolitical, 103
George W. Bush, 39, 88
global, 9, 10, 14, 15, 20, 23, 31, 61, 80, 82, 83, 87, 91, 95, 96, 97, 98, 103, 119, 125, 126, 127, 142, 143, 144, 145, 147, 149, 154, 155, 156, 157, 158, 159, 162
globalization, 10, 17, 22, 77, 127, 132, 140, 142, 143, 145, 147, 151, 152
globalizing, 142, 145

government, 36, 79, 85, 86, 91, 93, 99, 100, 102, 119, 126, 127, 133, 156, 159
greed, 165, 170
gross national product, 146

H

health care, 10, 14, 15, 22, 42, 56, 82, 89, 90, 91, 92, 93, 94, 95, 96, 98, 116, 129
health problems, 91, 92
hierarchy, 52, 66, 122, 123
Hillary Clinton, 42
Hiroshima and Nagasaki, 77, 88
Hispanic, 116
historical perspective, 13, 19, 22, 53, 67, 79, 108, 112
Hitler, 41, 78, 88
Holy wars, 124
homophobic, 46
human behavior, 38, 41, 43, 66, 135
human body, 107
human development, 17, 69, 83, 170
human history, 19, 20, 27, 28, 35, 38, 62, 68, 74, 77, 78, 99, 108, 121, 122, 123, 159
human needs, 93, 96, 155
human physiology, 67
human potential, 19, 23, 127, 170
human relations, 20, 136, 137
human rights, 80, 86, 121, 124, 126, 133, 139, 145, 159
human suffering, 13, 129

humanitarian, 19, 20, 21, 23, 72, 94, 129, 160, 168
humanity, 7, 13, 17, 20, 21, 32, 35, 42, 77, 78, 79, 86, 88, 89, 93, 96, 97, 99, 126, 133, 137, 150, 155, 163, 168, 170
hunger, 20, 94, 98, 125, 128, 129, 158, 162
hypocrisy, 73, 83, 111

I

ignorance, 14, 15, 17, 39, 76, 79, 108, 163
immigration, 98, 159, 160, 161, 162
immoral leaders, 126
imperialism, 124, 147, 149, 154
imports, 146
independence, 77, 137
industrialization, 46, 51, 61, 63, 65, 66
industries, 23, 83, 92, 132, 142, 150
infant mortality, 61
information revolutions, 146
inhumane, 76
innocent American, 79, 157
innovation, 103, 128, 146
institutionalized, 53
insurance, 15, 23, 89, 90, 91, 92
Intellectual, 17, 143, 149, 155
intellectual property rights, 143, 146
intelligence, 20, 46, 98, 130
internal combustion, 103, 148
international aide, 144

international community, 78, 82, 86, 119, 125, 126, 129, 133
international law, 125, 126, 133
international organizations, 144, 147
intervention, 15, 116, 117, 119, 156
intimidation, 85, 126
intolerance, 10, 104, 111
Iraq, 39, 79, 80, 118, 156, 157
Iraqi civilians, 79
Islam, 22, 140
Israel, 125, 139

J

James Madison, 117
Jews, 78, 138, 141
jobs, 11, 64, 70, 97, 98, 101, 132, 137, 144, 162

L

labor, 24, 29, 31, 35, 46, 67, 96, 100, 101, 113, 114, 115, 131, 132, 145
languages, 83, 106
Latin America, 51, 52, 77, 102, 117
leadership, 17, 19, 23, 34, 42, 46, 47, 50, 54, 61, 62, 73, 87, 88, 104, 110, 122, 123, 141, 143, 155, 157, 169
learning, 68, 80, 83, 85, 109, 111, 131, 135, 168
legislation, 149, 151
liberty, 78, 86, 117

M

male behavior, 51, 157
male leaders, 23, 47, 72, 86
male-dominated, 9, 21, 25, 32, 33, 50, 54, 57, 59, 73, 79, 162, 169
male-oriented, 58, 163
malnutrition, 14, 92, 94, 95, 129, 130, 163
malpractice, 91
mankind, 23, 28, 95, 169, 170
manpower, 128, 170
Margaret Mead, 58
marital arrangements, 45
Mark Twain, 118
marriage, 45, 52, 60, 61, 66, 68
masculine, 28, 33, 34, 41, 42, 43, 44, 77, 85, 122, 123, 165
masculinity, 34, 35, 38, 41, 42, 43, 132
massacres, 88, 169
materialism, 10, 22, 135
maternal, 51, 138, 167
Mechanization, 55, 98
medicine, 31, 89, 90, 91, 95
men, 19, 20, 28, 30, 33, 34, 35, 36, 37, 38, 39, 40, 41, 44, 46, 47, 48, 50, 51, 54, 55, 56, 57, 58, 59, 60, 62, 63, 64, 65, 72, 73, 89, 96, 165, 169
Middle East, 28, 53, 58, 141
military, 9, 10, 13, 14, 15, 16, 21, 40, 60, 71, 76, 78, 98, 103, 116, 119, 122, 123, 124, 125, 127, 128, 129, 130, 133, 147, 148, 157, 162
misinformation, 14, 72, 84, 108, 159

modern societies, 53, 56, 57, 95, 137
modern world, 43, 95, 140
money, 15, 20, 21, 24, 44, 56, 57, 64, 87, 89, 91, 93, 97, 98, 103, 126, 127, 129, 131, 135, 136, 160, 170
monopolies, 152
monopoly, 52, 143, 150, 152
moral authority, 76, 86, 103, 105, 124, 125, 133
moral imperative, 93, 109
moral leaders, 22, 23, 86, 116, 122, 123, 138, 155, 158
moral standards, 138
Moringa, 94
Mother Theresa, 23, 24
motherhood, 30, 57, 65, 97, 170
mothers, 49, 73, 85, 138
motivation, 30, 89, 138, 161
mulato, 116
multicultural, 14, 156, 157
Multiculturalism, 156
Muslims, 78, 138, 141

N

Napoleonic Complex, 41, 79
national, 11, 14, 15, 16, 28, 49, 72, 77, 78, 80, 81, 82, 83, 87, 91, 92, 96, 111, 117, 122, 123, 126, 127, 130, 133, 135, 146, 149, 155, 157, 158, 159
nationalism, 10, 77, 78, 83, 117, 122, 123, 124, 126, 127, 134, 155

nations, 10, 15, 16, 17, 20, 21, 23, 28, 31, 32, 34, 37, 39, 47, 49, 50, 54, 65, 76, 77, 79, 90, 97, 100, 103, 117, 122, 123, 124, 125, 126, 127, 129, 130, 134, 135, 141, 142, 143, 155, 156, 157, 158
natural, 20, 25, 29, 35, 45, 47, 60, 95, 97, 108, 117
nature versus nurture, 55
Neil Postman, 83, 138
new generations, 33, 37, 43, 83, 156
North America, 112
nuclear, 43, 63, 125, 128, 149
nuclear arsenals, 128
Nuremberg Trials, 126
nurturing, 9, 10, 17, 19, 21, 23, 38, 49, 51, 53, 55, 85, 97, 141, 157, 162, 170
nutrition, 55, 81, 85, 91, 95

O

oil, 99, 102, 103, 157
Oswald, 169
overpopulation, 10, 14, 17, 66, 95, 97, 98, 159

P

Palestine, 139
paradigm, 9, 16, 21, 33, 37, 151, 154, 165
Parents, 91
paternalistic, 70, 71, 154
paternity, 67, 68, 74, 76

patriarchal, 32, 56, 73, 74
patriarchy, 54
peace, 7, 10, 13, 16, 21, 22, 24, 32, 75, 79, 83, 85, 110, 117, 122, 123, 124, 125, 126, 134, 135, 138, 139, 140, 141, 142, 159, 164
peaceful, 17, 19, 20, 21, 33, 58, 71, 76, 78, 122, 123, 128, 139, 141, 142, 156, 168
Pentagon, 121, 129
Peter Berger, 169
pharmaceutical, 15, 23, 89, 90, 92
philosophy, 39, 43, 59, 68, 88, 94, 134, 141, 170
physical characteristics, 30, 106, 108
physical constitution, 67
physical strength, 29, 30, 57, 61, 69
political interest, 170
political leaders, 16, 20, 23, 43, 54, 66, 79, 83, 85, 87, 97, 110, 111, 124, 140, 169
politicians, 85, 88, 92, 143, 156
pollution, 10, 11, 14, 97, 159
poor, 13, 89, 90, 96, 131, 155, 160, 161, 162
poverty, 10, 11, 13, 14, 17, 20, 21, 82, 96, 97, 98, 99, 101, 112, 119, 127, 128, 129, 130, 144, 158, 161
power, 14, 16, 20, 21, 23, 24, 29, 33, 36, 37, 39, 40, 43, 46, 50, 51, 52, 55, 56, 57, 58, 65, 68, 69, 71, 72, 74, 75, 76, 79, 83, 118, 119, 120, 121, 122, 123,

127, 140, 141, 145, 149, 155, 156, 157, 158, 170
pragmatic, 14, 23, 81, 90, 92, 93, 94, 103, 104, 131, 138, 144, 162
pregnancy, 30, 50, 61, 62, 68, 69
prejudiced, 49, 109
President, 14, 39, 77, 88, 92, 119, 120, 139, 140, 157
primitive, 31, 35, 36, 37, 43, 49, 55, 66, 67, 88, 167
productivity, 98, 102, 131, 170
profitability, 99, 100, 101
profits, 15, 23, 90, 99, 100
prognosis, 69
propaganda, 164
prostitution, 73
psychological barriers, 47
psychological consequences, 132
psychological phenomenon, 65
psychological restraint, 132
public opinion, 124
punishment, 113, 114, 115, 130, 131

Q

quality of life, 100, 137

R

race, 37, 55, 61, 67, 78, 96, 97, 106, 109, 110, 111, 113, 114, 115, 116, 129
racism, 10, 14, 15, 17, 24, 44, 104, 105, 108, 109, 110, 111, 116, 135

rationalization, 88, 134, 141
rationalizations, 136
reason, 21, 31, 72, 73, 78, 102, 107, 119, 121, 122, 123, 128, 133
religion, 78, 111, 112, 138, 139, 140, 141, 164
religions, 10, 16, 22, 51, 81, 134, 138, 139, 140, 141, 158, 164
religious institutions, 22, 52, 168
religious leaders, 23, 45, 54, 83, 134, 135, 140, 158
repression, 72
reproductive systems, 39
research and development, 154
resources, 9, 13, 14, 15, 20, 21, 22, 25, 44, 91, 93, 94, 95, 97, 98, 103, 128, 129, 131, 144, 149, 155, 158, 162
responsibility, 55, 68, 85, 87, 112, 131, 132, 139
revolution, 29, 31, 39, 46, 56, 61, 69, 72, 98, 146, 148, 170
right to vote, 27
Roman Empire, 124, 147
Roman law, 148

S

Saddam Hussein, 79, 118, 119
Scandinavia, 28
Scandinavian countries, 50, 73, 98
school, 50, 77, 80, 81, 82, 83, 85, 87, 91, 159, 168
schools, 21, 39, 75, 82, 83, 84, 90, 116, 162
Scientific developments, 29, 72

sex roles, 27, 37, 38, 52, 56, 62, 64, 66, 67, 68, 69, 70, 72
sexism, 10, 13, 14, 17, 22, 27, 28, 31, 36, 38, 40, 44, 46, 48, 50, 73, 104, 135
sexual orientation, 45
slave, 113, 114, 115
social, 9, 10, 13, 14, 16, 17, 19, 21, 23, 24, 28, 29, 32, 33, 35, 37, 40, 43, 46, 47, 49, 51, 56, 58, 61, 62, 65, 66, 68, 69, 72, 77, 78, 92, 95, 96, 99, 100, 101, 102, 116, 117, 127, 131, 132, 135, 143, 145, 156, 168, 169, 170
social problems, 24, 92, 135, 169
socialist, 93, 137, 143, 159
socialization, 37, 54, 93
societies, 13, 14, 15, 16, 27, 28, 31, 34, 35, 37, 38, 40, 42, 45, 52, 56, 58, 59, 60, 62, 63, 65, 67, 69, 70, 72, 73, 74, 75, 76, 95, 96, 112, 136, 137, 141, 154, 156, 160
society, 23, 28, 29, 34, 36, 41, 42, 43, 44, 45, 46, 47, 49, 52, 53, 54, 57, 58, 60, 62, 63, 64, 65, 66, 71, 72, 73, 75, 84, 89, 92, 93, 102, 104, 105, 106, 108, 109, 110, 111, 112, 113, 114, 115, 116, 131, 132, 135, 136, 137, 138, 139, 142, 150, 155, 156, 157, 163, 165, 168
socio-economic, 67, 131, 143
sociological development, 113, 114, 115
sociology, 80, 168, 169

solutions, 9, 10, 14, 20, 22, 25, 80, 83, 90, 92, 94, 99, 102, 122, 123, 125, 135, 136, 159, 162, 163
sor Juana Ines de la, 72, 73
sovereignty, 16, 78, 127, 133
Status of Women, 35
stereotypes, 15, 34, 35, 36, 39, 41, 48, 50, 60, 63, 109, 116
stereotyping, 27, 51, 108, 113, 114, 115
students, 77, 80, 81, 83, 84, 85, 90, 91, 138
superiority, 45, 47, 51, 62, 147, 164
survival, 24, 29, 55, 62, 67, 70, 96, 133, 137, 142, 144, 156
Sweden, 64, 73, 107

T

taxes, 92, 117
teacher, 84, 138, 144
technological development, 64
technological developments, 31, 50, 97
technological society, 66, 136
technologies, 75, 102, 144, 145, 146, 147, 149, 150, 152, 153
technology, 9, 21, 22, 23, 32, 55, 56, 59, 61, 64, 69, 70, 82, 83, 92, 97, 102, 103, 122, 123, 140, 143, 146, 147, 148, 149, 150, 151, 152, 153, 154, 155, 158, 162
Teilhard de Charden, 168
the Golden Rule, 71
The Golden Rule, 22, 170

third world, 17, 34, 37, 50, 58, 95, 96, 97, 143, 151
third-world countries, 96, 154
Thomas Jefferson, 86, 110
Time magazine, 54
tolerance, 10, 45, 52, 138, 139, 140, 141, 142
traditional ideology, 66
traditional male mentality, 43
traditional mentality, 79
traditional sex-roles, 49

U

U.S. government, 76, 79, 86, 118, 119
U.S. role, 77
unemployment, 10, 82, 98, 137, 162
UNICEF, 24, 128
United States, 4, 14, 16, 24, 27, 28, 31, 32, 39, 46, 50, 56, 61, 67, 78, 79, 86, 87, 96, 101, 102, 103, 116, 117, 118, 120, 121, 122, 123, 124, 125, 127, 128, 130, 135, 148, 149, 156, 157, 159, 160, 161, 162, 164, 170
United States of America, 4, 27, 31, 32, 121, 159, 160, 162
universal health, 91, 98
urbanization, 63

V

values, 10, 17, 22, 30, 38, 43, 44, 53, 58, 62, 66, 67, 78, 117, 118, 134, 135, 136, 137, 139, 140, 141, 142, 145, 153, 157, 158
violence, 19, 20, 21, 25, 39, 78, 79, 83, 97, 121, 122, 123, 126, 130, 132, 138, 141, 142
violent, 20, 33, 51, 78, 83, 124, 132, 133, 135, 139, 141, 142
virginity, 52, 68, 74

W

Wal-Mart, 155
waste, 13, 15, 82, 91, 103, 129, 170
weapons, 13, 20, 21, 23, 40, 43, 60, 79, 103, 119, 125, 128, 130, 157, 162
Western culture, 53, 74, 142, 156
Western Culture, 169
white, 32, 105, 107, 111, 112
womankind, 170
women, 7, 13, 19, 23, 24, 27, 28, 29, 30, 32, 33, 34, 35, 36, 37, 39, 40, 41, 44, 45, 46, 47, 49, 50, 51, 52, 53, 55, 56, 57, 58, 60, 61, 62, 63, 64, 65, 68, 69, 71, 72, 73, 74, 75, 77, 96, 102, 129, 133, 139, 140, 165
World Bank, 102
world population, 95
World Trade Organization, 143, 144, 146
world's problems, 14, 21, 23, 73, 162

CPSIA information can be obtained at www.ICGtesting.com
Printed in the USA
LVOW08s1840170315

430918LV00001B/168/P